Everyday Mathematics®

Home Connection Handbook

A Guide for Teachers and Administrators

Grades 4 – 6

McGraw Hill Wright Group

Acknowledgements
Gary Cannon
Janice L. Haake
Heather Lash
Dr. Kathleen McCord
Wesley Sanders-Gosselink
Jan Widing

Photo Credits
Teacher and Administrator photos supplied by Wright Group.

Illustrations
Elizabeth Allen, pp. 47, 61; Anthology, p. 110.

www.WrightGroup.com

 **Wright Group**

Printed in the United States of America.

Send all inquiries to:
Wright Group/McGraw-Hill
P.O. Box 812960
Chicago, IL 60681

ISBN 0-07-604596-X

5 6 7 8 9 POH 13 12 11 10 09 08 07

The McGraw-Hill Companies

Welcome to *Home Connection Handbook*

This handbook is a collection of practical ideas, suggestions, and reproducible masters to support teachers and administrators in their ongoing communication with families. The teachers and administrators whose suggestions appear in this book have told us that reaching out to help families understand and appreciate their children's mathematics program is well worth the effort. With encouraging and supportive families, your students will be positive and successful, and your job will be more enjoyable.

To provide teachers and administrators with specific information relevant to their needs, this handbook is divided into four sections.

We hope the ideas and materials in this handbook will help you build strong partnerships with families by providing ways for them to learn about the *Everyday Mathematics* program philosophy, experience the activities and routines, and see evidence of their children's successes.

Teacher Ideas for Family Communication

Many teachers feel that ongoing communication with families is the key to gaining their support. When parents are supportive of a program, students respond to it positively. The following pages contain ideas "from the field" for communicating with families. Some suggestions are simple and easy, while others require more planning and time. The reproducible masters that follow these ideas for family communication make up the bulk of this section and support the ideas described.

Teacher Ideas

School Events

Welcoming families into your classroom with a Back-to-School Night or Open House is a good way to introduce *Everyday Mathematics*. Later in the year, consider holding a grade-level or school-wide Family Math Night where families have a chance to experience a variety of activities firsthand. If daytime events are better for your community, the Portfolio Day is another way to keep families connected.

Back-to-School Night

Hold this event within the first few weeks of school to provide a general overview of the curriculum for your grade.

▷ **Purpose:** Share key features of the program and the content emphasized for the year.

▷ **Helpful to have**

- Program components to show or display *(Teacher's Lesson Guide, Student Math Journal, Student Reference Book*, sample copies of Study Links, CDs, game kits, and *Content by Strand* Poster)

- Hand-out, transparency, or chart of the following:

  - *Everyday Mathematics* in the Classroom, p. 15
  - A copy of Presenter's Notes for *Everyday Mathematics* in the Classroom, pp. 16 and 17
  - Contend Emphasized in *Everyday Mathematics*, pp. 19–21

Open House

Most schools hold this event sometime during the first quarter to showcase students' learning and accomplishments during that period.

▷ **Purpose:** Share daily work, products from activities, and a game that allows students to demonstrate their mathematics skills.

▷ **Helpful to have**

- At least one math-related display (photos or products, (pp. 10 and 11)

- Math journals (Consider having students mark specific pages with stick-on notes—their favorite problems, their most challenging problems, and so on.)

- Products saved from a project, with student's written explanations

- Directions and materials for one math game students can play with family members

Family Math Night

Because Family Math Nights are such fun, interactive ways to teach families about *Everyday Mathematics*, some schools hold several throughout the year. Schedule your event for a less hectic time of year, such as January or February. Pages 59–65 provide planning support and suggestions.

▷ **Purpose:** Convey the value of games, enable students to share their learning, trace a strand across grade levels, and address questions.

▷ **Helpful to have**

♦ Several displays of "math in action" (pp. 10 and 11)

♦ Hands-on stations for games, activities, or technology (pp. 60 and 61)

♦ One station or time period to address common questions about the program

♦ A "thanks-for-attending" gift, such as a Parent Handbook (p. 8), Fact Triangles, deck of cards, and so on

"I teach algorithms to parents in 1-hour sessions. I ask them to pretend that they are students. I try to get them to experience first-hand how much fun students have learning mathematics."

Kathleen Burke
Math Coordinator
The Woods Academy
Bethesda, MD

Portfolio Day (daytime)

If your students have created portfolios, a daytime event during which they share their work with their families is ideal for the second quarter.

To keep the classroom from being crowded and noisy, most teachers schedule 4 or 5 families to attend in 30-minute time slots. Students guide their families through their portfolios in a designated area while classmates do other work. With ample preparation, students can share their portfolios with very little teacher supervision.

▷ **Purpose:** Give students the opportunity to share and reflect on their learning with their families.

▷ **Helpful to have**

♦ Portfolio contents organized in chronological order

♦ Completed Portfolio Reflection sheet (p. 66)

♦ A feedback sheet (stapled inside portfolio), on which family members can write comments to their children

Things to Send Home

Sending home math-related materials on a regular basis helps maintain good communication with families. Vary the form it takes—not all families have the time or the inclination to read lengthy informative pieces, but they do enjoy seeing their children's work or playing a game with their children at home.

▷ Family Letters and Study Links

Family Letters explaining the contents of each unit appear in the Study Link section of your *Math Masters* book. The first Family Letter is especially helpful as it gives a general overview of the program. While parents like to see their children practicing skills with Study Links pages, avoid parental frustration and do not assign pages that students cannot do on their own. If you think students can do the work with a reminder from the day, let them take home their math journals and refer to it for help.

▷ Classroom Newsletters

Consider having students write articles on recent learning topics and accomplishments. Become familiar with the masters in this book and use one as an attachment every now and then, such as: an explanation of a routine or algorithm (pp. 23–37), How to Help Your Child with Mathmathics (pp. 46 and 47), or the Literature List (pp. 54–57). Clip out a timely Frequently Asked Question (pp. 42–45) and paste it into your newsletter before you photocopy your class set. Be sure to attach the invitations to volunteer or to observe a math lesson (pp. 67 and 68) from time to time.

▷ Game Kits and Feedback Sheets

If your school has not purchased the *Everyday Mathematics* Family Games Kits, enlist the help of volunteers to make games kits that students can take home. Attach a Game Feedback sheet (p. 67) to each game to increase family participation.

> *"In our community, which is 80% Native American, we strive to give students ownership of their learning. This helps us with family support and 'buy-in'. We take time to play games during class, knowing that when students work together and teach others their retention increases. Then we create math game packets to send home. The students love being the 'experts' when they play the games with their families."*

Jenni Snyder
Elementary School Teacher
Lapwai School District
Lewiston, ID

▷ *Student Reference Book*

Allow students to take their *Student Reference Books* home on certain days, or have several copies available for check out. Let reading the *Student Reference Book* with a family member count toward any nightly reading requirements.

▷ **Journal Pages to Review and Sign**

Develop a system for sending math journals home for students to share with their families. Before students take their journals home, have them draw signature and date lines at the end of the section for a family member to review.

▷ **Interesting Problems**

Send home a problem which stimulated an interesting discussion or generated different solution strategies. Have students explain the problem or solutions to a family member, and then the family member can write a paragraph describing his or her response.

"When I send home the Individual Profiles of Progress for each unit, I have children write and complete the following prompts at the bottom of the page: In this unit, I had trouble with _____. I liked learning about _____. I want to learn more about _____. *The responses provide valuable insight for me and for the parents."*

**Stefanie Trammell
Math Coach/
Elementary School
 Teacher
MSD of Perry Township
Indianapolis, IN**

Parent Handbook

Many teachers or schools create an informational handbook as an at-home *Everyday Mathematics* resource for parents. The pages in the reproducible section and the suggestions below will help you create your own customized Parent Handbook.

How to Create

▷ **Photocopy and staple:** Create a cover featuring a title, your name, the school's name and contact information. Make copies of selected pages from this handbook and staple the pages along the edge.

▷ **Three-hole punch:** If your budget allows, punch holes in the copies and put them in a three-pronged folder. This enables you to send additional pages home throughout the year.

What to Include

▷ **Administrator's introductory letter:** If this is your first year of program implementation, it is especially helpful to include a letter explaining the reasons for adopting *Everyday Mathematics*.

▷ **Personal introductory letter:** Write your own letter encouraging parents to freely and regularly give you feedback.

▷ **Pages from this handbook:** Consider including your grade level's content chart (pp. 19–21), How to Help Your Child with Mathematics (pp. 46 and 47), Algorithms in *Everyday Mathematics* (pp. 28–37), the games list (p. 58), and the pages on routines (pp. 23–26).

When to Distribute

▷ **Back-to-School Night or Open House:** If your community seems anxious for material, make your Parent Handbook available early in the year. However, receiving this kind of resource before the program has really gotten underway could overwhelm some parents.

▷ **Family Math Night:** Consider using the handbook as a "free gift" for attending!

▷ **Conferences:** Have a copy of the Parent Handbook ready for each family. Review the contents of the handbook with parents so they can confidently help their children.

> *"**At the** first parent-teacher conference in August, teachers meet with parents one on one to discuss the content their children will learn throughout the year and address any concerns or questions. When discussing mathematics, teachers give parents the "Parents' Guide to* Everyday Mathematics" *handbook. This guide provides a nice overview of the program, including the routines, and gives the parents an at-home reference. In November, conferences focus on first trimester performance and grades."*
>
> **John Themelis**
> **Educational Assistant /**
>   **Co-Math Leader**
> **Albuquerque Public Schools**
> **Albuquerque, NM**

Parents in the Classroom

Inviting parents into your classroom to either lend a hand or observe will help develop their appreciation for *Everyday Mathematics*. This experience will be most worthwhile for the parents, the students, and you with some advance planning on your part.

▷ Scheduled Visits

To encourage classroom visits, have parents use the forms on pages 67 and 68 to schedule a time to volunteer in the classroom or to observe.

▷ Specific Duties for Volunteers

Do everything you can to make volunteers feel productive and helpful. Have all necessary materials (including game or activity directions) in a basket or box. Use the form on page 69 to let volunteers know which students they'll work with and what your goals are for the activity.

▷ Tasks for Observers

Familiarize observers with the lesson flow by giving them a handout of An *Everyday Mathematics* Lesson (p. 22). Ask them to look for something specific, such as the ways students learn from each other, the multiple ways a concept is presented, the kinds of questions you ask, or the fact practiced during game play. Having a focus for their visit gives observers something to discuss afterward.

*"**Parents who** work full time and cannot volunteer in your classroom might like to help in other ways. Read the Advance Preparation section of your* Teacher's Lesson Guide *and then invite parents to help with cutting and preparing for future lessons."*

Jessica Colella
Elementary School
    Teacher
Oak Park School
    District 97
Oak Park, IL

▷ Follow-up

After parents observe the class, debrief by asking a few open-ended questions either in person or later by phone: *What did you notice? Anything interesting? Do you have questions? Any feedback?* This shows you value their insights.

▷ Volunteer Appreciation

Thank all volunteers and observers for their time. The fact that parents rearrange their schedules and find childcare for their other children shows enormous commitment to their children's education. Also, let your principal know when a parent has volunteered or observed so that he or she can acknowledge this effort.

Displays

Because the *Everyday Mathematics* program is based on activities and interactions rather than textbooks, you can use displays to communicate the excitement of the program more effectively than written material. Visual displays are especially helpful for families whose native language is not English. Think creatively about all the surfaces you might use as display space: bulletin boards, tables, counters, walls, doors, shelves, and wires strung between walls.

Teacher Ideas

▷ *Everyday Mathematics* Materials

If this is your first year of implementation, families will be curious about the program's materials. At your Back-to-School Night or Open House, display your *Teacher's Lesson Guide,* a *Student Math Journal*, the *Student Reference Book*, *Content by Strand* Poster, a tool kit, and a Family Games kit. Attach a large, self-sticking note to each item to describe how it is used. For example, on the math journal you might write:

- ◆ Used daily by students
- ◆ Stays in class
- ◆ Record of student's mathematical understanding

You may also want to set up a computer station to show families the iSRB and the *Everyday Mathematics* Online Games or the *Everyday Mathematics* Games CD.

▷ Photographs

Use a bulletin board or album to display photos of students playing games, doing projects, discussing solutions, and showing off their products. Add a title to identify the activity featured in the photos, and have students write captions.

With a digital camera, you or your students can post photos on a class or school Web site. Students can also send photos to math pen pals at a partner *Everyday Mathematics* school. Digital images are easy to incorporate into your classroom newsletter. Older students like being asked to write articles or captions to accompany the photos.

> *"I cover my walls with things the children can refer to when they need help. For example, I create an Everyday Mathematics word wall for mathematics vocabulary. Each new word is posted with a drawing of the concept. I maintain our Number Museum and continue to add things throughout the year. I also display posters of diagrams used in the program, such as the parts-and-total diagram, along with questions students can ask themselves when working the diagram. This is a great display for children and parents."*

Marisol Carrillo
Elementary School
  Teacher
Orange County Public
  Schools
Orlando, Florida

▷ Products from Daily Lessons

Daily lessons produce many products that, when displayed, speak a great deal about what students are learning. Post students' number stories, name-collection boxes, and "What's My Rule?" exercises, on a bulletin board; or better yet, bind them together into class books that can be displayed or circulated.

Many Projects have products that serve as lasting artifacts of the experience. Have students write about how they made them, and display the explanations along with the products.

▷ Museums

In several units over the course of the year, students create thematic math "museums." After your class has completed museum-related lessons, relocate the museum to a more public location, such as a library or hallway bulletin board. The collections created by students are often informative and interesting to adults and to other students in the school.

▷ Timely Topics

Especially during the first year of implementation, families will have questions about *Everyday Mathematics*. Create bulletin boards to display program approaches that might be unfamiliar to them. Use a question, such as "What Is an Algorithm?" as the title of a bulletin board. In the case of this question, display algorithms students have invented along with "traditional" algorithms. The week you first display a topic bulletin board would be a good time to attach a handout to your classroom newsletter, such as pages 28–37, Algorithms in *Everyday Mathematics*.

▷ Math-related Literature

One goal of home communication is to help families consciously integrate math activities into their daily lives. Encourage reading books about mathematics at home by creating a display of several books recommended in the Literature List on pages 54–57. While it is best to have the actual books on display, you can also post color photocopies of the book jackets on a bulletin board.

*"**We took** digital pictures of the students creating angles, parallel lines, triangles, reflex angles, and angles within a clock. Then we created a bulletin board with the pictures, titled "What is Your Angle?", to display students' thinking."*

Maryann Diglio
Elementary School
Teacher
Staten Island
Academy
Staten Island, NY

Parent-Teacher Conferences

Conferences are opportunities for parents and teachers to communicate about individual student progress. In addition, conferences can be an ideal time to solicit feedback about *Everyday Mathematics*, answer questions about the philosophy or content, and share information. Have a variety of materials on hand to provide a broad picture of *Everyday Mathematics* and each student's progress.

▷ Records and Observations

Remember to stress that students develop mathematical skills at different rates. Any of these items will help you share information about students' progress:

- Individual Profiles of Progress
- Progress Checks
- Products from lessons and activities (especially journals)
- Anecdotal records
- Portfolio Reflection sheet, filled out by student (p. 66)

▷ Communication

Parents may often come to a conference with questions and opinions. It is helpful to let them clear their minds before discussing their children with you. Begin with a general question, such as *How do you think math is going for your child?* and listen attentively to the responses. If there are questions you cannot address, make a note to have your principal follow up with the parents and let them know that this will happen.

> *"Because* Everyday Mathematics *is different from math programs that parents know, we find that student-led conferences are a great way to inform parents. The students go over their math journals and discuss their strengths and the areas they want to improve upon. Students also show examples of their work and demonstrate some of the algorithms they are working on. The kids really take ownership of their learning."*
>
> Carleen Baldwin
> Elementary School
>   Teacher
> Lapwai School
>   District
> Lewiston, ID

▷ **Information Table**

Have a few handouts available on a table in the hallway or waiting area. Consider making copies of How to Help Your Child with Mathematics (pp. 46 and 47), explanations of routines (pp. 23–25), Do-Anytime Activities (pp. 48–53), the games list (p. 58) or Algorithms in *Everyday Mathematics* (pp. 28–37). If an information table isn't an option, you can give helpful handouts to parents during your conference.

▷ **Displays of work**

When discussing a student's performance in mathematics, it can help parents to be aware of the range of work being produced in a classroom and the various ways students solve problems. A bulletin board featuring recent work in the class can give parents a picture of their children's mathematical environment.

▷ **Student Participation**

Some teachers find it extremely worthwhile to have students attend and participate in their own conferences. Most students are amazingly insightful when it comes to evaluating their learning, and they tend to feel more ownership when involved in conferences. If students have collected work in portfolios, it is especially appropriate for them to reflect on selected pieces with their parents.

"I send home the Individual Profile of Progress after each Progress Check to let families know what their children still need to work on and what their strengths are. At parent-teacher conferences, I go over the profiles again, adding information gathered from more recent observations, journal pages, and Math Boxes. Individual Profiles of Progress are great tools for documenting progress!"

Amy Santos
Elementary School
　Teacher
Leeward School District
Ewa Beach, HI

▷ **Help at Home**

Conferences are the perfect time to suggest a few ways parents can help their children with math at home. You will want to remind parents of the importance of Family Letters and Study Links. Have an example of each of these on hand to review their important features. Or, you may want to share two or three examples from How to Help Your Child with Mathematics (pp. 46 and 47) or Do-Anytime Activities (pp. 48–53). If your school holds math workshops for parents, be sure to mention this and encourage them to attend.

Teacher Masters for Family Communication

The materials in this section will help you carry out the ideas and strategies described on pages 3–13. Most of these pages are intended for you to copy and give to families, but you may also wish to use the masters as models for materials you write yourself.

To assist you with distributing these reproducible forms,
please look for one of the following icons at the top of each page.

 For your reference   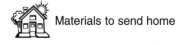 Materials to send home

Everyday Mathematics in the Classroom

Background

- Developed by the University of Chicago School Mathematics Project

- Based on research about how students learn and develop mathematical power

- Provides the broad mathematical background needed in the 21st century

In *Everyday Mathematics* you can expect to see...

...a problem-solving approach based on everyday situations;

...an instructional approach that revisits concepts regularly;

...frequent practice of basic skills, often through games;

...lessons based on activities and discussion, not a textbook; and

...mathematical content that goes beyond basic arithmetic.

Presenter's Notes

The following chart is a resource for you to use when discussing *Everyday Mathematics* with families. It is meant to be paired with *Everyday Mathematics* in the Classroom on page 15.

Presentation Text	Notes
Background ♦ Developed by the University of Chicago School Mathematics Project ♦ Based on research about how students learn and develop mathematical power ♦ Provides the broad mathematical background needed in the 21st century	♦ *Everyday Mathematics* was extensively researched and field tested in classrooms before publication. It was also written one grade at a time. ♦ Students learn mathematics best through hands-on activities that build on their interests and connect to their experiences. ♦ Young students can grasp mathematics concepts traditionally saved for older students (for example, algebra) when concepts are explored with concrete materials and pictures. ♦ Careers now require the ability to access, evaluate, and use information to solve problems. Rote memorization and basic arithmetic (computation) are not enough.
In *Everyday Mathematics* you can expect to see… …a problem-solving approach based on everyday situations;	♦ Students learn mathematics skills while solving problems that interest them. ♦ Explaining solutions and strategies to each other is one way students learn. ♦ Students are encouraged to solve problems in multiple ways, creating flexibility of thinking.
…an instructional approach that revisits concepts regularly;	♦ The program moves briskly and revisits key ideas and skills in slightly different contexts throughout the year. ♦ Multiple exposure to topics ensures solid comprehension. ♦ Strands are woven together—no strand is in danger of being left out. ♦ Mastery is developed over time. The *Content by Strand* Poster depicts the interwoven design. ♦ Homework problems will have familiar formats, but different levels of difficulty.

Presentation Text	Notes
…frequent practice of basic skills, often through games;	◆ Frequent practice is necessary to recall facts with accuracy and speed. Students of all ability levels find math games a fun way to practice. ◆ Focus is on understanding concepts behind basic facts, as well as mastering the facts themselves. ◆ Games are essential to the program, not optional or extra. ◆ Games are assigned as homework. (Families should expect to play!)
…lessons based on activities and discussions, not a textbook; and	◆ Students record, organize, and demonstrate their learning in a math journal. ◆ Focus is on the learning process—most written material is aimed at the teacher. ◆ Students use a variety of math tools. ◆ *Student Reference Book* contains information related to lesson content and game rules.
…mathematical content that goes beyond basic arithmetic.	◆ Students receive instruction in all major areas of mathematics: number sense, data analysis, geometry, measurement, algebra, and probability. ◆ Strands are not taught in isolation. They are interwoven with other strands in a "real world" way. (Example: students may graph the weight of different animals and find the difference in weight between the most and the least heavy.)

How Students Learn in *Everyday Mathematics*

Think about the master chefs you see on television—how do they acquire their knowledge and skills? No one starts out chopping onions at high speed, inventing their own dishes, or running a restaurant! Chefs develop their cooking expertise over time, starting with basic skills and easy recipes. Gradually, they practice those skills, learn important food science concepts, and gain experience by cooking in many different restaurants.

In a similar way, *Everyday Mathematics* is based on the idea that students build understanding and develop skills as a result of many meaningful and connected learning experiences. Mastery of mathematics concepts and skills comes with repeated exposure and practice, not after just one lesson. This enables students to make new connections and build on the mathematical content they already know while gradually learning more difficult and challenging content. Think of this process as climbing a spiral staircase—with each twist of the stairs, the previous steps can be seen, but you are farther and higher.

To help students develop mastery, you may notice that the mathematical content in this program is taught in a repeated fashion, first with informal exposure and then through more formal and directed instruction. For example, students will have many different hands-on experiences with algebra—they will draw and act out number stories, write number sentences, find missing information in Frames-and-Arrows diagrams, and graph functions before they begin to explore variables in algebraic functions.

The design of *Everyday Mathematics* allows students to gain a more genuine understanding of mathematical concepts, a much more solid mathematical foundation, and exposure to the entire scope of mathematics each year.

How can you help? Because homework is one way students revisit concepts, you can support your child by helping with Study Links and playing math games at home when they are assigned.

Content Emphasized in Grade 4

In *Everyday Mathematics*, students develop a broad background by learning concepts and skills in these six content strands. The fourth-grade program emphasizes the following content.

Number and Numeration
Reading, writing, and using whole numbers, fractions, decimals, percents, and negative numbers; exploring scientific notation

Operations and Computation
Practicing addition and subtraction to proficiency; developing multiplication and division skills; exploring addition, subtraction, multiplication, and division methods; inventing individual procedures and algorithms; experimenting with calculator procedures

Data and Chance
Collecting, organizing, displaying, and interpreting numerical data

Measurement and Reference Frames
Exploring metric and U.S. customary measures; linear, area, volume, and weight; exploring geographical measures; using numbers in reference frames; number lines; coordinates; times and dates; latitude and longitude

Geometry
Developing an intuitive sense about 2-dimensional and 3-dimensional objects, their properties, uses, and relationships

Patterns, Functions, and Algebra
Designing, exploring, and using geometric and number patterns; reading, writing, and solving number sentences

For a lesson-by-lesson view of the way students learn this content, see the Grade 4 *Content by Strand* Poster.

Content Emphasized in Grade 5

In *Everyday Mathematics*, students develop a broad background by learning concepts and skills in these six content strands. The fifth-grade program emphasizes the following content.

Number and Numeration
Recognizing place value in numerals for whole numbers and decimals; expressing numbers in scientific notation; finding factors of numbers; comparing properties of prime and composite numbers; representing rates and ratios with fraction notation

Operations and Computation
Extending whole-number facts with addition, subtraction, multiplication, and division to fractions and decimals; evaluating symbolic expressions

Data and Chance
Collecting, organizing, and analyzing data using bar graphs, line graphs, circle graphs, and stem-and-leaf plots

Measurement and Reference Frames
Using linear, area, capacity, and personal reference measures; locating items with reference to an origin or zero point, for example, ordinal numbers, times of day, dates, and temperatures

Geometry
Investigating angles and rotations; calculating area and volume; drawing to scale; introducing relationships of 2-dimensional and 3-dimensional figures; exploring new transformations that affect attributes of geometric shapes

Patterns, Functions, and Algebra
Determining divisibility; exploring number patterns; applying formulas to geometric figures; creating number models; working with scientific calculators; squaring and unsquaring numbers; exploring variables in formulas

For a lesson-by-lesson view of the way students learn this content, see the Grade 5 *Content by Strand* Poster.

Content Emphasized in Grade 6

In *Everyday Mathematics*, students develop a broad background by learning concepts and skills in these six content strands. The sixth-grade program emphasizes the following content.

Number and Numeration
Recognizing place value in whole numbers and decimals; using exponential and scientific notation; finding factors and multiples; converting between fractions, decimals and percents; ordering positive and negative numbers

Operations and Computation
Solving problems involving whole numbers, fractions, decimals, and positive and negative numbers; applying properties of addition, subtraction, multiplication, and division

Data and Chance
Collecting, organizing, displaying, and analyzing data; identifying and comparing landmarks of data sets (mean, median, mode, and range); using probability to represent and predict outcomes and analyze chance

Measurement and Reference Frames
Measuring using metric and U.S. customary units; using formulas to calculate area, circumference, and volume; naming and plotting points on a coordinate grid

Geometry
Measuring and drawing angles; understanding properties of angles; identifying and modeling similar and congruent figures; constructing figures with a compass and straightedge; drawing to scale; exploring transformations of geometric shapes; experimenting with modern geometric ideas

Patterns, Functions, and Algebra
Creating and extending numerical patterns; representing and analyzing functions; manipulating algebraic expressions; solving equations and inequalities; working with Venn diagrams; applying algebraic properties; working with ratios and proportions

For a lesson-by-lesson view of the way students learn this content, see the Grade 6 *Content by Strand* Poster.

An *Everyday Mathematics* Lesson

Most daily lessons in *Everyday Mathematics* follow the structure below. In each lesson, there are warm-up activities, focused instructional time, and activities that provide practice and review of skills already learned. This review is essential for developing and maintaining skills.

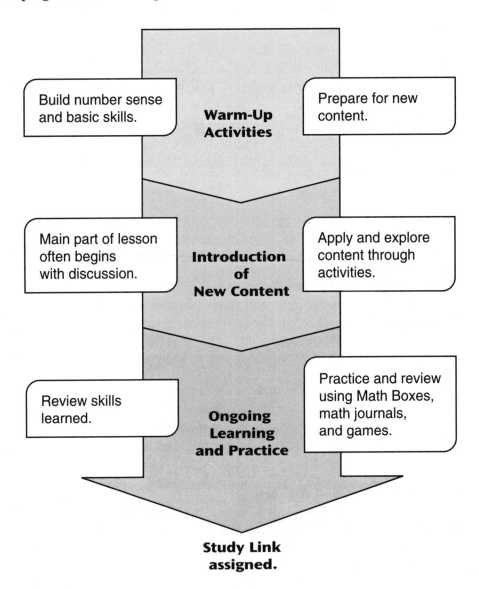

Build number sense and basic skills.

Prepare for new content.

Warm-Up Activities

Main part of lesson often begins with discussion.

Apply and explore content through activities.

Introduction of New Content

Review skills learned.

Practice and review using Math Boxes, math journals, and games.

Ongoing Learning and Practice

Study Link assigned.

Lesson plans always include options for meeting the needs of different types of learners. A teacher may choose to work with small groups or with individuals who would benefit from support in the form of previewing lesson content, providing multiple avenues for acquiring skills, extending concepts, or developing English language abilities.

Routines: Name-Collection Boxes

Name-collection boxes are one of many routines students work with regularly in *Everyday Mathematics*. A routine is a familiar, predictable activity that provides ongoing practice in a skill or content area.

Students use name-collection boxes to develop the idea that there are many equivalent names for one number. Because arithmetic, for the most part, involves replacing numbers or expressions with equivalent numbers or expressions (we replace $5 + 7$ with 12 or $\frac{1}{2}$ with $\frac{1}{4} + \frac{1}{4}$) this is an important concept for students to understand.

All name-collection boxes feature a label attached to a box with lines for writing. The idea is to fill the box with different names for the number on the label. Numbers can be named using one or more operations (addition, subtraction, multiplication, and division), words in any language, tally marks, arrays, Roman numerals, and so on.

These two examples show the variety and range of thinking students use to creatively express equivalent names.

14
1,400%
$2 * 7$
$\frac{1}{4}$ of 56
$20 - 6$
$1 + 13$
700/50
$3^3 - 13$
$0.028 * 500$
XIV
$(3 * 7) - 7$

16
half of 32
$116 - 100$
8 twos
$(2 \times 5) + 6$
sixteen
10 less than 26
XVI
$32 \div 2$
4^2
$4 + 4 + 4 + 4$

Beginning in fourth grade, *Everyday Mathematics* introduces a simpler and more compact name-collection box like the ones above.

Routines: "What's My Rule?"

"What's My Rule?" is one of many routines students work with regularly in *Everyday Mathematics*. A routine is a familiar, predictable activity that provides ongoing practice in a skill or content area. The type of thinking students do when working with this routine prepares them for sucess with algebra.

In "What's My Rule?" problems, there is a diagram that represents an imaginary "function machine." The machine takes in a number, applies a rule, and puts out a new number. A table is used to keep track of "in" and "out" numbers.

To solve a "What's My Rule?" problem, some missing information (the "in" numbers, the "out" numbers, or the rule) must be found using the information that is given. Beginning in fifth grade, variables are sometimes used as input numbers. Here are several examples and ways to help your child find the missing information.

1. **The output numbers are missing.** The rule and the input numbers are given. Have your child say or write the input number and the rule as an equation, such as "$39 + 10 = ?$" Write the sum in the "out" column of the table.

in	out
39	
54	
163	

```
  39
  in
   ↓
┌──────────┐
│ Rule     │
├──────────┤
│ +10      │
└──────────┘
     ↓
    out
     ?
```

Solution: The output numbers are 49, 64, and 173.

2. **The input numbers are missing.** The rule and the output numbers are given. Students use different approaches to solving this kind of problem. Your child may want to find the "in" number by thinking, "$? - 6 = 6$," or perhaps want to think of the machine in reverse, such as "$6 + 6 = ?$"

in	out
	6
	10
	20

```
   ?
  in
   ↓
┌──────────┐
│ Rule     │
├──────────┤
│ −6       │
└──────────┘
     ↓
    out
     6
```

Solution: The input numbers are 12, 16, and 26.

3. The rule is missing. The input and output numbers are given. Have your child look at the first pair of numbers in the table. Ask *How can you get from 55 to 60?* Have your child suggest a rule; then try the rule with the next pair of numbers. Find a rule that works with all the pairs.

in	out
55	60
85	90
103	108

```
    55
    in
     ↓
    ⎏⎐
  ┌──────────┐
  │ Rule     │
  ├──────────┤
  │ ?        │
  └──────────┘
         ⎏⎐
          ↓
         out
         60
```

Solution: The rule is add 5 (or plus 5, or +5)

4. Sometimes the rule and some of the numbers are missing. In a problem like the following one, ask *Which information can help you find the rule?* Use the two pairs of input and output numbers to find the rule. Once the rule is found, the missing numbers in the table can be found.

in	out
6	16
0	10
26	
	53

```
     ?
    in
     ↓
    ⎏⎐
  ┌──────────┐
  │ Rule     │
  ├──────────┤
  │ ?        │
  └──────────┘
         ⎏⎐
          ↓
         out
          ?
```

Solution: The rule is add 10. The output number is 36; the input number is 43.

Routines: Fact Triangles

Fact Triangles are one of many routines students work with regularly in *Everyday Mathematics*. A routine is a familiar, predictable activity that provides ongoing practice in a skill or content area.

Being able to recall basic number facts, such as 7 + 6 or 8 * 8, with speed and accuracy is called *fact power*. Fact power is an important part of learning mathematics, and it involves frequent practice. In addition to the games and short exercises students do in class, they also use Fact Triangles to practice and master basic number facts.

Fact Triangles are the *Everyday Mathematics* version of flash cards. Because Fact Triangles are based on *fact families*, they help students memorize facts more effectively than flash cards. Fact families are sets of related facts that link either addition and subtraction or multiplication and division. These examples show several Fact Triangles and the fact families they model.

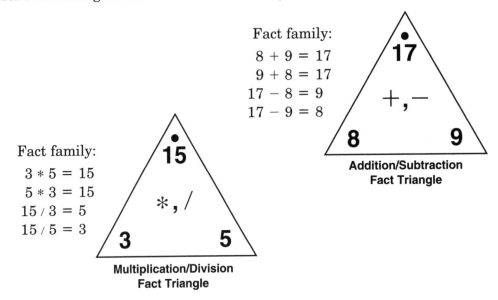

Fact family:
8 + 9 = 17
9 + 8 = 17
17 − 8 = 9
17 − 9 = 8

17

+ , −

8 **9**

Addition/Subtraction Fact Triangle

Fact family:
3 * 5 = 15
5 * 3 = 15
15 / 3 = 5
15 / 5 = 3

15

∗ , /

3 **5**

Multiplication/Division Fact Triangle

It is best to practice Fact Triangles with a partner. One person covers one corner with a finger, and the person practicing gives a number fact that has the covered number as the answer. For this triangle, the fact would be "9 − 3 = 6."

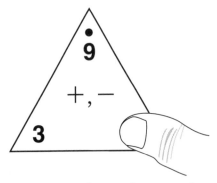

9

+ , −

3

This simple game makes it easy for students to play at home. Fact Triangles are often recommended in Study Links.

Mathematical Reflexes

In *Everyday Mathematics*, developing good mental arithmetic skills is an important part of becoming a flexible problem solver. In fact, some of these skills should become so automatic that they can be used almost without thinking; such skills are called *reflexes*.

The most important of these reflexes is the ability to recall the basic addition, subtraction, multiplication, and division facts. In *Everyday Mathematics* students build and maintain strong mental-arithmetic skills, or *fact power*, through frequent and varied practice. Opportunities for practice include:

♦ **Fact families and Fact Triangles:** sets of related basic facts linked by either addition and subtraction or multiplication and division (such as $3 * 5 = 15$, $5 * 3 = 15$, $15 / 3 = 5$, and $15 / 5 = 3$). Fact families can be practiced using Fact Triangles, the *Everyday Mathematics* version of flash cards.

♦ **Daily warm-ups and Math Boxes problem sets:** regular activities built into daily lessons

♦ **50-fact Multiplication Drills:** one-minute multiplication facts drills for fourth graders

♦ **Games:** the predominant format for practice. Games can be tailored for different skill levels and engage students in a fun activity that would otherwise be tedious.

Students in Grades 1 and 2 begin developing fact power by mastering the addition and subtraction facts. By the end of Grade 4, students are expected to be well on their way to mastering multiplication and division facts.

By the end of Grade 6, students should have obtained fact power and have well-grounded, automatic responses in these key reflexes:

♦ Rounding, estimating, and doing simple mental arithmetic;

♦ Computing with 10, 100, 1,000, and other powers of 10;

♦ Finding equivalent names for fractions;

♦ Identifying equivalencies between important "everyday" fractions, decimals, and percents; and

♦ Manipulating symbols in algebraic expressions and equations.

With a firm grasp of mathematical reflexes, students enjoy confidence and success at higher levels of mathematics.

Algorithms in *Everyday Mathematics*

What is an algorithm?

An algorithm is a well-defined procedure or set of rules guaranteed to achieve a certain objective. You use an algorithm every time you follow the directions to put together a new toy, use a recipe to make cookies, or defrost something in the microwave.

In mathematics, an algorithm is a specific series of steps that will give you the correct answer every time. For example, in grade school, you and your classmates probably learned and memorized a certain algorithm for multiplying. Chances are, no one knew why it worked, but it did!

In *Everyday Mathematics*, students first learn to understand the mathematics behind the problems they solve. Then, quite often, they come up with their own unique working algorithms that prove that they "get it." Through this process, they discover that there is more than one algorithm for computing answers to addition, subtraction, multiplication, and division problems. Having students become comfortable with algorithms is essential to their growth and development as problem solvers.

How do students learn to use algorithms for computation?

Ideally, students should develop a variety of computational methods and the flexibility to choose the procedure that is most appropriate in a given situation. *Everyday Mathematics* includes a variety of standard computational algorithms, as well as students' invented procedures. The program leads students through three phases as they learn each mathematical operation (addition, subtraction, multiplication, and division).

Algorithm Invention

In the early phases of learning an operation, students are encouraged to invent their own methods for solving problems. This approach requires students to focus on the meaning of the operation. They learn to think and use their common sense, as well as new skills and knowledge. Students who invent their own procedures:

- learn that their intuitive methods are valid and that mathematics makes sense.

- become more proficient with mental arithmetic.

- are motivated because they understand their own methods, as opposed to learning by rote.

- become skilled at representing ideas with objects, words, pictures, and symbols.

- develop persistence and confidence in dealing with challenging problems.

Alternative Algorithms

After students have had many opportunities to experiment with their own computational strategies, they are introduced to several algorithms for each operation. Some of these algorithms may be the same or similar to the methods students have already invented on their own. Others are traditional algorithms which have commonly been taught in the U.S. or simplifications of those algorithms. And others are entirely new algorithms that have significant advantages in today's technological world.

Students are encouraged to experiment with various algorithms and to become proficient with at least one.

Demonstrating Proficiency

For each operation, the program designates one alternative algorithm as a "focus" algorithm. Focus algorithms are powerful, relatively efficient, and easy to understand and learn. They also provide common and consistent language, terminology, and support across grade levels of the curriculum.

All students are expected to learn and demonstrate proficiency with the focus algorithm. Once they can reliably use the focus algorithm, students may use it or any alternative they prefer when solving problems. The aim of this approach is to promote flexibility while ensuring that all students know at least one reliable method for each operation.

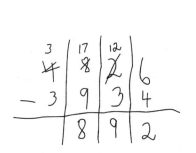

trade-first subtraction with columns

trade-first subtraction with an unnecessary trade

Addition Algorithms

This section presents just a few of the possible algorithms for adding whole numbers.

Focus Algorithm: Partial-Sums Addition

You can add two numbers by calculating partial sums, working one place-value column at a time, and then adding all the sums to find the total.

> ### Example: Partial-Sums Addition
>
> ```
>                                        268
>                                      + 483
> Add the hundreds (200 + 400).          600
> Add the tens (60 + 80).                140
> Add the ones (8 + 3).                + 11
> Add the partial sums (600 + 140 + 11). 751
> ```

Column Addition

To add using the column-addition algorithm, draw vertical lines to separate the ones, tens, hundreds, and so on. Add the digits in each column, and then adjust the results.

For some students, the above process becomes so automatic that they start at the left and write the answer column by column, adjusting as they go without writing any of the intermediate steps. If asked to explain, they might say something like this:

> ### Example: Column Addition
>
> Add the digits in each column.
>
> | hundreds | tens | ones |
> |---|---|---|
> | 2 | 6 | 8 |
> | + 4 | 8 | 3 |
> | 6 | 14 | 11 |
>
> Since 14 tens is 1 hundred plus 4 tens, add 1 to the hundreds column, and change the number in the tens column to 4.
>
> | hundreds | tens | ones |
> |---|---|---|
> | 2 | 6 | 8 |
> | + 4 | 8 | 3 |
> | 7 | 4 | 11 |
>
> Since 11 ones is 1 ten plus 1 one, add 1 to the tens column, and change the number in the ones column to 1.
>
> | hundreds | tens | ones |
> |---|---|---|
> | 2 | 6 | 8 |
> | + 4 | 8 | 3 |
> | 7 | 5 | 1 |

"200 plus 400 is 600. But (looking at the next column) I need to adjust that, so I write 7. 60 and 80 is 140. But that needs adjusting, so I write 5. 8 and 3 is 11. With no more to do, I can just write 1."

Opposite-Change Rule

If you add a number to one part of a sum and subtract the same number from the other part, the result remains the same. For example, consider:

$$8 + 7 = 15$$

Now add 2 to the 8, and subtract 2 from the 7:

$$(8 + 2) + (7 - 2) = 10 + 5 = 15$$

This idea can be used to rename the numbers being added so that one of them ends in zeros.

Example: Opposite-Change Rule

Rename the first number and then the second.

$$
\begin{array}{c c c}
\xrightarrow{\text{Add 2.}} & \xrightarrow{\text{Add 30.}} & \\
268 & 270 & 300 \\
+\ 483 & +\ 481 & +\ 451 \\
\xrightarrow{} & \xrightarrow{} & 751 \\
\text{Subtract 2.} & \text{Subtract 30.} &
\end{array}
$$

Rename the second number and then the first.

$$
\begin{array}{c c c}
\xrightarrow{\text{Subtract 7.}} & \xrightarrow{\text{Subtract 10.}} & \\
268 & 261 & 251 \\
+\ 483 & +\ 490 & +\ 500 \\
\xrightarrow{} & \xrightarrow{} & 751 \\
\text{Add 7.} & \text{Add 10.} &
\end{array}
$$

Subtraction Algorithms

There are even more algorithms for subtraction than for addition, probably because subtraction is more difficult. This section presents several subtraction algorithms.

Focus Algorithm: Trade-First Subtraction

This algorithm is similar to the traditional U.S. algorithm except that all the trading is done before the subtraction, allowing children to concentrate on one thing at a time.

Example: Trade-First Subtraction

Examine the columns. You want to make trades so that the top number in each column is as large as or larger than the bottom number.

hundreds	tens	ones
9	3	2
− 3	5	6

To make the top number in the ones column larger than the bottom number, borrow 1 ten. The top number in the ones column becomes 12, and the top number in the tens column becomes 2.

hundreds	tens	ones
	2	12
9	~~3~~	~~2~~
− 3	5	6

To make the top number in the tens column larger than the bottom number, borrow 1 hundred. The top number in the tens column becomes 12, and the top number in the hundreds column becomes 8.

hundreds	tens	ones
	12	
8	~~2~~	12
~~9~~	~~3~~	~~2~~
− 3	5	6

Now subtract column by column in any order.

hundreds	tens	ones
	12	
8	~~2~~	12
~~9~~	~~3~~	~~2~~
− 3	5	6
5	7	6

Counting Up

To subtract using the counting-up algorithm, start with the number you are subtracting (the subtrahend), and "count up" to the number you are subtracting from (the minuend) in stages. Keep track of the amounts you count up at each stage. When you are finished, find the sum of the amounts.

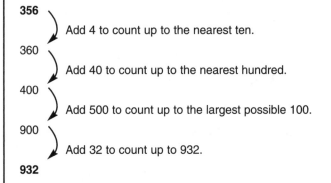

Example: **Counting Up**

To find 932 − 356, start with 356 and count up to 932.

356
    Add 4 to count up to the nearest ten.
360
    Add 40 to count up to the nearest hundred.
400
    Add 500 to count up to the largest possible 100.
900
    Add 32 to count up to 932.
932

Now find the sum of the numbers you added.

```
      4
     40
    500
  +  32
    576
```

So, 932 − 356 = 576.

Left-to-Right Subtraction

To use this algorithm, think of the number you are subtracting as a sum of ones, tens, hundreds, and so on. Then subtract one part of the sum at a time.

Example: **Left-to-Right Subtraction**

To find 932 − 356, think of 356 as the sum 300 + 50 + 6. Then subtract the parts of the sum one at a time, starting from the hundreds.

```
                            932
Subtract the hundreds.    − 300
                            632

Subtract the tens.        −  50
                            582

Subtract the ones.        −   6
                            576
```

Same-Change Rule

If you add or subtract the same number from both parts of a subtraction problem, the results remain the same. Consider, for example:

$$15 - 8 = 7$$

Now add 4 to both the 15 and the 8:

$$(15 + 4) - (8 + 4) = 19 - 12 = 7$$

Or subtract 6 from both the 15 and the 8:

$$(15 - 6) - (8 - 6) = 9 - 2 = 7$$

The same-change rule algorithm uses this idea to rename both numbers so the number being subtracted ends in zeros.

Example: **Same-Change Rule**

Add the same number.

$$
\begin{array}{r} 932 \\ -\ 356 \end{array}
\xrightarrow{\text{Add 4.}}
\begin{array}{r} 936 \\ -\ 360 \end{array}
\xrightarrow{\text{Add 40.}}
\begin{array}{r} 976 \\ -\ 400 \\ \hline \end{array}
$$

Subtract. 576

Example: **Same-Change Rule**

Subtract the same number.

$$
\begin{array}{r} 932 \\ -\ 356 \end{array}
\xrightarrow{\text{Subtract 6.}}
\begin{array}{r} 926 \\ -\ 350 \end{array}
\xrightarrow{\text{Subtract 50.}}
\begin{array}{r} 876 \\ -\ 300 \\ \hline \end{array}
$$

Subtract. 576

Partial-Differences Subtraction

The partial-differences subtraction algorithm is a fairly unusual method, but one that appeals to some students.

The procedure is fairly simple: Write partial differences for each place, record them, and then add them to find the total difference. A complication is that some of the partial differences may be negative.

Example: **Partial-Differences Subtraction**

$$
\begin{array}{r} 932 \\ -\ 356 \\ \hline \end{array}
$$

Subtract 100s.	900 − 300	600
Subtract 10s.	30 − 50	− 20
Subtract 1s.	2 − 6	− 4
Add the partial differences.		576

Multiplication Algorithms

Students' experiences with addition and subtraction algorithms can help them invent multiplication algorithms. For example, when estimating a product mentally, many students begin to compute partial products: "Ten of these would be. . ., so 30 of them would be. . ., and we need 5 more, so. . ." Beginning in *Third Grade Everyday Mathematics*, this approach is formalized as the partial-products multiplication algorithm. This algorithm and others are discussed in this section.

Focus Algorithm: Partial Products

To use the partial-products algorithm, think of each factor as the sum of ones, tens, hundreds, and so on. Then multiply each part of one sum by each part of the other, and add the results.

Rectangular arrays can be used to demonstrate visually how the partial-products algorithm works. The product 14 * 23 is the number of dots in a 14-by-23 array. The diagram below shows how each of the partial products is represented in the array.

> **Example: Partial Products**
>
> To find 67 * 53, think of 67 as 60 + 7 and 53 as 50 + 3. Then multiply each part of one sum by each part of the other, and add the results.
>
> | | |
> | --------------------- | -----: |
> | | 67 |
> | | * 53 |
> | Calculate 50 * 60. | 3,000 |
> | Calculate 50 * 7. | 350 |
> | Calculate 3 * 60. | 180 |
> | Calculate 3 * 7. | + 21 |
> | Add the results. | 3,551 |

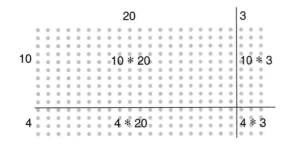

$$14 \times 23 = (10 + 4) * (20 + 3)$$
$$= (10 * 20) + (10 * 3) + (4 * 20) + (4 * 3)$$
$$= 200 + 30 + 80 + 12$$
$$= 322$$

Modified Repeated Addition

Many students are taught to think of whole-number multiplication as repeated addition. However, using repeated addition as a computation method is inefficient for anything but small numbers. For example, it would be extremely tedious to add fifty-three 67s in order to compute 67 * 53. Using a modified repeated addition algorithm, in which multiples of 10, 100, and so on, are grouped together, can simplify the process.

> **Example: Modified Repeated Addition**
>
> Think of 53 * 67 as fifty 67s plus three 67s.
> Since ten 67s is 670, fifty 67s is five 670s.
> So, 53 * 67 is five 670s plus three 67s.
>
> | |
> | ----: |
> | 67 |
> | * 53 |
> | 670 |
> | 670 |
> | 670 |
> | 670 |
> | 670 |
> | 67 |
> | 67 |
> | 67 |
> | 3,551 |

Lattice Multiplication

Everyday Mathematics initially included the lattice method for its recreational value and historical interest (it has been used since A.D. 1100 and appeared in the first printed arithmetic book, published in 1478) and because it provided practice with multiplication facts and adding single-digit numbers. This method has become a favorite of many students in *Everyday Mathematics*.

The following example shows how the method is used to find 67 * 53.

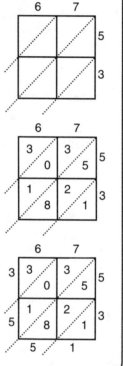

Example: **Lattice Multiplication**

Follow these steps to find 67 * 53.

- Draw a 2-by-2 lattice, and write one factor along the top of the lattice and the other along the right. (Use a larger lattice to multiply numbers with more digits.)

- Draw diagonals from the upper-right corner of each box, extending beyond the lattice.

- Multiply each digit in one factor by each digit in the other. Write each product in the cell where the corresponding row and column meet. Write the tens digit of the product above the diagonal and the ones digit below the diagonal. For example, since 6 * 5 = 30, write 30 in the upper-left box with the 3 above the diagonal and the 0 below.

- Starting with the lower-right diagonal, add the numbers inside the lattice along each diagonal. If the sum along a diagonal is greater than 9, carry the tens digit to the next diagonal.

  The first diagonal contains only 1, so the sum is 1. The sum on the second diagonal is 5 + 2 + 8 = 15. Write only the 5, and carry the 1 to the next column. The sum along the third diagonal is then 1 + 3 + 0 + 1, or 5. The sum on the fourth diagonal is 3.

- Read the product from the upper left to the lower right. The product is 3,551.

Division Algorithms

One type of division situation involves making as many equal-size groups as possible from a collection of objects: How many dozens can you make with 746 eggs? How many 5-passenger cars are needed for 37 people? Such problems ask, "How many of these are in that?" More generally, a / b can be interpreted as "How many bs are in a?" This idea forms the basis for the division algorithms presented in this section.

Focus Algorithm: Partial Quotients

The partial-quotients algorithm uses a series of "at least, but less than" estimates of how many bs are in a.

Example: Partial Quotients

Estimate the number of 12s in 158.

You might begin with multiples of 10 because they are simple to work with. There are at least ten 12s in 158 (10 * 12 = 120), but there are fewer than twenty (20 * 12 = 240). Record 10 as a first estimate, and subtract ten 12s from 158, leaving 38.

```
12)158      10    first guess
   120
    38       3    second guess
    36
   ___     ____
     2      13    sum of guesses
```

$$158 / 12 \longrightarrow 13 \text{ R2}$$

Now estimate the number of 12s in 38.

There are more than three (3 * 12 = 36) but fewer than four (4 * 12 = 48). Record 3 as the next estimate, and subtract three 12s from 38, leaving 2.

Since 2 is less than 12, you can stop estimating. The final result is the sum of the estimates (10 + 3 = 13) plus what is left over (the remainder of 2).

Column Division

Column division is a simplification of the traditional long division algorithm you probably learned in school, but it is easier to learn. To use the method, you draw vertical lines separating the digits of the divisor and work one place-value column at a time.

Example: Column Division

To find 683 / 5, imagine sharing $683 among 5 people. Think about having 6 hundred-dollar bills, 8 ten-dollar bills, and 3 one-dollar bills.

First, divide up the hundred-dollar bills. Each person gets one, and there is one left over.

```
     1  |     |
  5)6    |  8  |  3
  - 5    |     |
     1  |     |
```

Trade the leftover hundred-dollar bill for 10 ten-dollar bills. Now you have a total of 18 ten-dollar bills. Each person gets 3, and there are 3 left over.

```
     1  |  3  |
  5)6    |  8̸  |  3
  - 5    | 18  |
    1̸    | -15 |
         |  3  |
```

Trade the 3 leftover ten-dollar bills for 30 one-dollar bills. You now have a total of 33 one-dollar bills. Each person gets 6, and there are 3 left over.

```
     1  |  3  |  6
  5)6    |  8̸  |  8̸
  - 5    | 18  | 33
    1̸    | -15 | -30
         |  3̸  |  3
```

So, when you divide $683 among 5 people, each person gets $136, and there are $3 left over. So, 683 / 5 = 136 R3.

Problem Solving

What is problem solving?

In *Everyday Mathematics*, problem solving means much more than doing calculations and finding answers to printed "word problems." While the idea of problem solving does include number stories (word problems), it also includes working with problems for which the solution methods are not known in advance. Think of it this way: a problem is not a genuine problem if the problem solver knows exactly what to do right away!

Here are two examples of mathematical problems.

> - *A store sells a certain brand of cereal in two sizes: a 10-ounce box that costs $2.50 and a 15-ounce box that costs $3.60. Which box is the better buy? Why?*
>
> - *This is an up-and-down staircase that is 5 steps tall. How many squares are needed for an up-and-down staircase that is 10 steps tall?*
>
>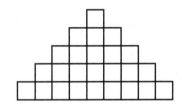

Different students might use different approaches to solve the problems above. For the staircase problem, for example, students might use blocks, make a drawing, look for and describe a pattern, or write a number model to come up with an answer. *Everyday Mathematics* focuses on four basic ways of looking at, or representing, problems: concrete, verbal, pictorial, and symbolic.

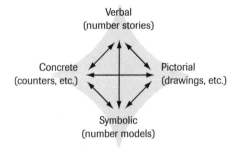

The program aims to not only develop students' comfort and skill with all the representations, but also to develop their abilities to translate between the representations. Symbolic representations (including number models with variables) and pictorial representations with graphs become increasingly important in Grades 4–6.

Why is problem solving important?

Learning to solve problems is the principal reason for studying mathematics. When students are able to use their skills and understanding to solve real world problems, they begin to see mathematics as something meaningful, useful, and even exciting.

Furthermore, the demands for mathematics competence and problem-solving ability are continually increasing in our world. Desirable careers require people to work collaboratively and apply their knowledge to unfamiliar, complex situations. *Everyday Mathematics* prepares students for the future by involving them in problem-solving situations that develop their skills in group interaction, communication, and the use of mathematical tools.

How is problem solving taught?

Problem solving is a complex process. This diagram shows how people often think about problem solving with everyday situations.

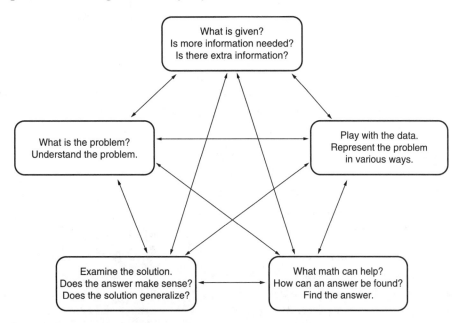

Students develop the skills needed to navigate among the different parts of the problem-solving process through the following kinds of activities.

♦ **practicing specific parts of the process separately:** Students practice many specific skills that are useful in solving problems, such as counting, measuring, calculating, estimating, looking up information, and so forth.

♦ **creating and solving number stories:** Students work with real, age-appropriate problems that involve numbers and a question. They gradually progress from learning to make up their own number stories to writing number models that use variables to fit their stories.

♦ **sharing strategies and solutions:** Students develop the ability to think, strategize, and use common sense by discussing both their correct and incorrect problem-solving strategies with the teacher and classmates.

Assessment in *Everyday Mathematics*

Throughout *Everyday Mathematics*, there are many opportunities to collect information about students' abilities. The purpose of gathering this information is to:

♦ see how each student's mathematical understanding is developing; and

♦ provide feedback to the teacher about each student's instructional needs.

The process of collecting information to track each student's progress and make decisions about how and what to teach is known as *assessment*. An assessment plan is an essential part of every effective educational program.

A Balance of Assessments

Students show what they know and can do in different ways. For this reason, teachers have a variety of assessment tools and techniques from which to choose. It is important to gather information not only about students' procedural skills, but also their understanding of concepts. *Everyday Mathematics* provides opportunities for students to demonstrate their learning through ongoing assessment and periodic assessment, and many schools use external assessment as well.

Ongoing Assessment

This is often called *informal assessment* because information is collected from the ordinary work that students do every day in mathematics class. Teachers use observation and students' products (work) to look for specific indicators of learning.

♦ *Observation* involves watching what students do and say during oral exercises, slate routines, discussions, strategy sharing, and game play. Teachers take notes or mark checklists to keep track of important information.

♦ *Product assessment* involves collecting and reviewing samples of daily work. Examples of students' work include Math Boxes, pages from a math journal, written explanations and diagrams (often done on an Exit Slip at the end of a lesson), and record sheets from games. These products may be saved in a student's portfolio—a collection of selected work intended to show progress over time.

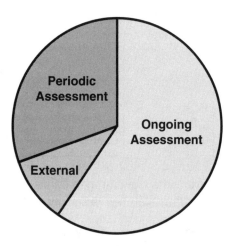

Periodic Assessment

Often called *formal assessment*, these are special assessment events that occur at the end of each unit (called *Progress Checks*), the middle of the year, and the end of the year. These more formal assessments use a combination of observation and products as well.

◆ *Observation* involves noting students' responses, either spoken or written on a slate, to questions the teacher asks aloud.

◆ *Product assessment* uses information from three different kinds of written products:

• *Self Assessment*, which asks students to evaluate their own progress;

• *Written Assessment*, which uses a format similar to a standard test; and

• *Open Response*, which focuses on students' ability to use their mathematical understanding to solve complex problems and explain their solution strategies.

External Assessment

Many schools, districts, or states mandate other tests to measure the progress of their students at regular intervals, such as Grade 3, Grade 5, Grade 8 and so on. These tests vary widely, from traditional standardized tests with multiple-choice responses to more performance-based assessments.

How Can Parents Support Assessment?

As a parent, you can support the assessment process by communicating with your child's teacher on a regular basis. Teachers communicate with parents by sending home a Family Letter to explain the contents of each unit and Study Links pages to review and practice material learned in lessons.

You can do your part by letting the teacher know what your child says about mathematics and how your child is doing with homework assignments. Ask yourself some of these questions to better pinpoint your child's progression with mathematics. Has your child been more interested in math? Is there something your child doesn't quite "get"? Can your child do the Study Links independently, or do you need to help a great deal? How much time does your child typically spend on a Study Links assignment? When you play math games or talk about real-life math situations at home, what do you notice about your child?

Families have unique insights about their children that are important to share with teachers. This information, when shared, can help teachers form a more complete picture of each student's development and adjust lessons to meet specific needs.

Frequently Asked Questions

Teacher Note: Cut and paste these questions into your newsletter or send one home along with appropriate student work.

Question: How will students practice and learn basic facts?

Answer: Students will learn and practice all of the basic facts in many different ways without having to complete an overwhelming number of drill pages. They will play mathematics games, work with Fact Triangles, and take part in short oral drills to review facts as a group. Students also use Addition/Subtraction and Multiplication/Division Fact Tables to practice facts and keep a record of the facts they have learned.

Question: Why are students using calculators? Will they become dependent on the calculator for solving problems?

Answer: In *Everyday Mathematics*, students use calculators to learn concepts, recognize patterns, develop estimation skills, and explore problem solving. They learn that a calculator can help them solve problems beyond their current paper-and-pencil capabilities; they also learn that, in some situations, they can use their own problem-solving abilities to get an answer more quickly than they can with a calculator. Students learn to use their basic facts and operations knowledge and estimation skills to decide whether the calculator's solution is reasonable. Students do not become dependent on calculators. Instead, they become comfortable and skillful users of a practical technological tool.

Question: How does *Everyday Mathematics* prepare students for standardized tests?

Answer: *Everyday Mathematics* prepares students for standardized tests through activities that strengthen the skills needed for success on these tests and familiarize them with the standardized test format. Students take timed tests and multiple-choice tests, play games that reinforce basic facts, frequently discuss and analyze problem-solving strategies, and learn ways to check the reasonableness of an answer. Throughout the program, students explain their thinking and reasoning in writing, which prepares them for the extended response questions that are becoming increasingly significant on state tests. And because the program distributes instruction among all the mathematics strands and continually revisits topics, students approach standardized tests without gaps in their basic knowledge.

Question: What is the purpose of Math Boxes? Why aren't the problems related?

Answer: Math Boxes are one way *Everyday Mathematics* provides students with continuous practice and review of *all* mathematical content. Almost every lesson includes a Math Boxes page in the math journal as part of the Ongoing Learning and Practice section of the lesson. The problems on a Math Boxes page provide practice in various skills and concepts learned up to that point. This way, students don't forget what they have learned, and they maintain and even improve their skills. Math Boxes are designed as independent activities, but at the beginning of the year, some guidance may be needed. Teachers often use Math Boxes to make informal assessments of students' progress.

Question: How will my child develop strong computation skills?

Answer: Students gain the fact knowledge they need for computation from basic facts practice, which consists of playing mathematical games, working with Fact Triangles, using fact tables, and taking part in short oral drills to review as a group. They develop an understanding of the need for computation, which operations to use, and how to use those operations by solving problems through number stories about real-life situations. They are given the opportunity to invent and use their own algorithms to solve problems, which they share and explain to their classmates. They also practice mental arithmetic and do activities that encourage rounding and estimating numbers mentally. All of these activities help students compute with accuracy and speed.

Question: Why do students play games during mathematics lessons?

Answer: *Everyday Mathematics* games reinforce concepts in a valuable and enjoyable way. They are designed to help students practice their basic facts and computation skills and develop increasingly sophisticated strategies. For example, some games give students experience using a calculator, while other games emphasize the relationship between the money system and place value. Games also lay the foundation for learning increasingly difficult concepts.

Students are often asked to play *Everyday Mathematics* games with family members as part of their home practice. As you learn to play the games yourself, you will begin to understand some of the ways games help students learn mathematics.

Question: Why does my child have to move on to the next lesson if he or she hasn't mastered skills in the current lesson?

Answer: *Everyday Mathematics* is based on the idea that mastery of mathematics concepts and skills comes with repeated exposure and practice, not after just one lesson. To help students develop mastery, mathematical topics are introduced in an informal way, and then presented numerous times in different contexts with gradually more formal, directed instruction. When students revisit topics, they make new connections and gain different insights. Students regularly review and practice new concepts through activities, games, and assignments. This gives them sufficient time to internalize and master the concepts and skills that are the designated goals for their specific grade level.

Question: Why does my child learn different algorithms to solve problems?

Answer: When students first begin learning about computation, they spend a lot of time experimenting with a variety of algorithms and sharing their own problem-solving methods. Instead of simply memorizing a set of prescribed algorithms, they learn to think, use common sense, and understand the purpose of algorithms. They are then required to demonstrate proficiency in one focus algorithm for each operation—addition, subtraction, multiplication, and division. Focus algorithms are powerful, relatively efficient, and usually easier to understand and learn than traditional algorithms. Once students have mastered the focus algorithm for each operation, they are free to use any method to solve problems.

Question: How will students with advanced math skills be challenged?

Answer: *Everyday Mathematics* is designed to move students beyond basic arithmetic and nurture their higher-order and critical-thinking skills. Many students who have mastered basic facts and certain methods of computation will be challenged to apply these skills to solving everyday, real-world programs. Because teachers use questions to stimulate thinking and drive discussions, mathematically-gifted students are challenged to think flexibly, articulate their understandings, and explain problem-solving strategies to their classmates. In addition, because the program is activity-based and has many open-ended activities, teachers can easily make modifications to increase the level of challenge. Throughout the lessons, there are options for enrichment, extension, and game variations, all of which can provide challenge to highly capable students. Finally, the breadth and depth of mathematics covered in the program, along with its brisk pacing, often provide challenges for students eager to explore topics such as algebra or data and chance.

Question: My child has special needs. How does the program address learning differences?

Answer: *Everyday Mathematics* offers many opportunities for teachers to meet the varying needs of each student. The program is flexible—that is, it is possible to adjust or modify most activities according to student needs, and teachers may include additional activities for the purpose of fine-tuning a concept, providing extra practice, or helping a student with a particular learning style. Lessons involve many open-ended activities that allow students to succeed at their own skill levels. Students develop their particular strengths and improve their weak areas by playing games, inventing algorithms, writing numbers stories, and solving problems in *5-Minute Math* and Math Boxes exercises. Teachers may group students in order to tailor instruction or an activity to meet the group's needs.

Question: How do you measure each student's progress? How do you know what each student has learned?

Answer: *Everyday Mathematics* teachers assess understanding periodically and on an ongoing basis. Teachers frequently make notes of students' progress while observing them working on Math Boxes or slate activities. Teachers also evaluate students' responses to *5-Minute Math*, interactions during group work or games, and written responses to Math Messages. There are Progress Checks for each unit and Mid-Year and End-of-Year assessments for evaluating individual student progress as well. Teachers maintain checklists to track each student's progress toward achieving specific Grade Level Goals. These records are used to determine whether certain topics need review and whether particular students need additional help or challenge.

Question: How does *Everyday Mathematics* prepare students for middle and high school mathematics?

Answer: *Everyday Mathematics* is designed around the principle that students build upon their existing knowledge as they progress through the grades. It is also designed to teach students concepts and skills in all strands of mathematics, not just arithmetic, with an emphasis on understanding and flexibility of thinking over rote memorization. The program takes students through the stages of working with mathematics in a mostly concrete, pictorial way to working in a more abstract and symbolic way. This approach allows students to complete the elementary school program with solid basic skills in mental arithmetic and algorithms and procedures. In addition, students have the ability to use these skills, along with their common sense, to solve complex problems and communicate their strategies and results. Students enter mathematics in the higher grades with a solid foundation in areas such as algebra and probability that have traditionally been left out of elementary school math programs.

How to Help Your Child with Mathematics

Create a homework routine.

Familiar routines help work go smoothly at school *and* at home. With your child, decide on a time and place to do homework, along with a few rules. A typical routine might go like this:

Come home, have a snack, clear a space at the table, start math homework. Create a place for homework supplies. Always have a sharp pencil, and circle problems you want help with. Once homework is complete, put it in your book bag.

Read Family Letters and Study Links.

These pages describe what your child is learning so that you can help. They also suggest fun, easy math activities you can do at home. Consider keeping all of these pages in a special folder to refer to later.

Communicate with the teacher.

You are the link between your child and school, and it is your responsibility to share your thoughts and concerns with the teacher. Call or write a note if your child has had trouble with homework, ask questions if you or your child do not understand something, and share good news when you see progress.

Ask your child to explain.

Encourage your child to teach you the day's math lesson by using the problems in the Study Links. Ask questions about the steps your child uses to solve a problem, such as *Why did you put that number there?* or *What does that zero mean?*

Use questions to help.

Although it's tempting to give children answers when they're confused, they learn more if you help them discover the answers for themselves. Try doing this with questions such as these:

♦ *Have you seen problems like this before? Is there an example anywhere that might help?*

♦ *What is the problem asking you to do or to find?*

♦ *What's one idea you have for finding an answer?*

♦ *Can you draw a picture of the problem? Can you use objects* (like coins, beans, and so on) *to show the problem?*

Be accepting of mistakes.

Let your child know that every mistake is an opportunity to learn. When your child makes a mistake, ask him or her to explain how he or she arrived at the answer, give praise for the correct steps or thinking, and gently point out where the error occurred. Then have your child try a similar problem (you may have to make one up) to practice the new understanding.

Play math games.

Games your child brings home from school or store-bought games that involve mathematical thinking will help your child master skills. Your child's teacher can give you a list of popular commercial games with mathematical content.

Observe a mathematics lesson in your child's classroom, or volunteer to help.

Visit your child's classroom—it's the best way find out more about *Everyday Mathematics*. When you volunteer to help with activities, you also learn a great deal. Do not worry if you're not a math expert—teachers always appreciate an extra hand and will find ways to use your skills.

Read the *Student Reference Book* with your child.

Many schools periodically send home this "math encyclopedia" for families and students to use together. Choose a page or section related to the day's Study Link, and read it together. Try the activities or questions at the end of the section with your child.

Share real-life math situations.

Think about the ways you use math in your everyday life—at work, at the store, at the bank, in the kitchen, and so on. Invite your child to observe or participate in these activities with you. Encourage your child to think mathematically about common activities, such as folding laundry or taking out the garbage—*How many socks are in 12 pairs? About how many pounds does a bag of trash weigh?*

Give gifts that encourage mathematical exploration.

Children love special gadgets and tools, as well as games and activities that challenge their minds. Giving a gift related to math is a good way to reinforce and reward your child's accomplishments. Here are some ideas: a watch, a timer, an hour glass (egg timer), a calendar, a tape measure, a calculator, pattern blocks, books of brainteasers, 3-dimensional building kits, puzzles, maps, and a wide variety of games.

Do-Anytime Activities for Grade 4

These activities are easy and fun to do with your child at home, and they will reinforce the skills and concepts your child is learning in school.

Unit 1	◆ Help your child identify real-world examples of right angles (the corner of a book) and parallel lines (railroad tracks). ◆ Have your child compile a shapes scrapbook or create a collage of labeled shapes. Images can be taken from newspapers, magazines, and photographs.
Unit 2	◆ Help your child look up the population and land area of the state and city in which you live, and compare these facts with those of other states and cities.
Unit 3	◆ Make up number sentences with correct and incorrect answers. Ask your child to put next to the sentence a "T" if the answer is correct and an "F" if the answer is incorrect. For example, try $5 * 6 = 35$ (F); $6 * 2 + 4 = 16$ (T); $4 * (2 + 5) = 13$ (F). ◆ Continue practicing multiplication and division facts by using Fact Triangles and fact families or by playing games from the *Student Reference Book*.
Unit 4	◆ Gather money from piggy banks or wallets. Ask your child to show you two different amounts, such as \$1.33 and \$4.20. Practice adding or subtracting the amounts. Your child can use a calculator to check the answers.
Unit 5	◆ Have your child write numbers through the millions and billions and practice reading them. Then select two and ask your child to tell which one is the greater number. ◆ Practice extended facts with your child. Start with $3 * 30$, $3 * 300$, and then try $3 * 3,000$. Have your child make up extended facts for you to calculate.
Unit 6	◆ Hide an object in a room of your house, and give your child directions for finding it. Your child can move only according to your directions, and the directions can be given only in fractions or degrees. For example, say "Make a $\frac{1}{4}$-turn and walk $3\frac{1}{2}$ steps. Now, turn 180° and walk 4 steps." Switch roles and have your child hide an object and give you directions to find it. ◆ Make a game of identifying and classifying angles: acute (less than 90°), obtuse (between 90° and 180°), right (90°), straight (180°), and reflex (between 180° and 360°) in everyday things (buildings, bridges, ramps, furniture).

Unit 7	◆ Encourage your child to recognize how probability is used in everyday situations, such as weather reports. Have your child make a list of things that could *never happen*, things that *might happen*, and things that are *sure to happen*.
Unit 8	◆ Have your child measure the perimeters of rooms in your house or of household objects. Then have him or her find the areas of the objects.
	◆ Help your child draw a scale map of your city, town, neighborhood, or have your child do a scale drawing of the floor plan of your home.
Unit 9	◆ Have your child look for everyday uses of fractions and percents. Look in games, grocery stores, cookbooks, measuring cups, and newspapers. When finding fractions, decimals, or percents, ask your child to change them from one form to another. For example, if you see "$\frac{1}{4}$ off", ask your child to tell what percent is equal to $\frac{1}{4}$ (25%).
	◆ Write whole numbers and decimals for your child to read, such as 650.02 (*six hundred fifty and two-hundredths*). Ask your child to identify the digits in the various places in the numbers—hundreds place, tens place, ones place, tenths place, and so on.
Unit 10	◆ Have your child look for repeating borders or frieze patterns (a design made of shapes that are in a line or lined up) on buildings, rugs, and floors. Your child may want to sketch the friezes or draw original patterns.
	◆ Use sidewalk chalk to make a number line with positive and negative numbers. Have your child solve addition and subtraction problems by walking on the number line. For example: to solve $-2 + 6$, your child would start on -2 and walk to the right six numbers to find the sum. Switch roles. For an inside activity, use paper, pencil, and fingers.
Unit 11	◆ Have your child find the volume of various rectangular prisms around your house, such as shoe boxes and fish tanks.
Unit 12	◆ During trips in the car, let your child know how far you will be traveling and the approximate speed you'll be moving at. Ask your child to estimate about how long it will take to get to your destination.
	◆ When grocery shopping, ask your child to help you find the "best buy" by comparing the cost per unit (ounce, gram, each) of different package sizes. For example, compare the cost of a family-size box of cereal with the cost of a regular-size box.

Do-Anytime Activities for Grade 5

These activities are easy and fun to do with your child at home, and they will reinforce the skills and concepts your child is learning in school.

Unit 1	◆ Ask your child to name as many factors as possible for a given number such as 24 (1, 24, 6, 4, 12, 2, 8, 3). To make sure the factors are correct, your child can multiply them with a calculator.
Unit 2	◆ Practice extending multiplication facts. Write each set of problems so that you child may recognize a pattern. Set A: 6 * 10 6 * 100 6 * 1,000; Set B: 5 * 10 5 * 100 5 * 1,000 ◆ When your child adds or subtracts multi-digit numbers, talk about the strategy that works best for him or her. Try not to impose the strategy that works best for you! Here are some problems to try: 467 + 343; 761 + 79; 894 − 444; 842 − 59.
Unit 3	◆ To learn more about population data and its uses, visit the Web site for the U.S. Bureau of the Census at www.census.gov. Have your child write three interesting pieces of information that he or she learned. ◆ Draw various angles: acute (less than 90°), obtuse (between 90° and 180°), and right (90°). Ask your child to estimate each angle measurement and then use a protractor to find the actual measurement. Compare the results. Switch roles, letting your child draw angles for you to estimate and measure.
Unit 4	◆ Find a map of your state and ask your child to use the scale to find the distance from a particular city to another city.
Unit 5	◆ Identify percents used in stores, newspapers, and magazines. Help your child find the sale price of an item that is discounted by a percent. For example, a $40 shirt discounted by 25% will cost $30. ◆ Practice writing numbers as a fraction and then as a decimal. Try one-fourth ($\frac{1}{4}$, 0.25), three-tenths ($\frac{3}{10}$, 0.3) and so on.
Unit 6	◆ Have your child practice adding fractional parts of a hour with a digital clock. Ask questions, such as "What time will it be an hour and a half from now? What was the time a quarter of an hour ago?" ◆ Practice adding and subtracting fractions with the same denominator.

Unit 7	◆ Create a number sentence that includes at least three numbers, several different operations, and parentheses. Have your child solve the number sentence. Then change the problem by placing the parentheses around different numbers. Ask your child to solve the new problem and explain how it changed according to the order of operations, for example, $(6 * 5) - 3 = 27$ and $6 * (5 - 3) = 12$.
	◆ Think of two numbers with exponents such as 2^5 and 3^3. Ask your child to determine which number is greater. If you like, check your child's answer on a calculator. Switch roles.
Unit 8	◆ Use a deck of cards to practice comparing fractions. Use only the number cards 2 through 9. Each player is dealt two cards and creates a fraction using one card as the numerator and one card as the denominator. The player with the greater fraction takes all four cards.
	◆ When at a store, reinforce percents by pointing out discounts and asking your child to figure out the sale price. If, for example, a sign shows "40% off", select an item, round the price to the nearest dollar, and help your child calculate the savings.
Unit 9	◆ Have your child draw a picture using rectangles, parallelograms, and triangles. Once completed, work together to find the area of each shape, and write it inside each shape. Ask your child, "What do you notice about the size of the area and the size of the shape?"
Unit 10	◆ Draw several circles and ask your child to find the radius, diameter, and circumference of each. Cut them out and make a design.
	◆ Practice evaluating simple algebraic expressions by asking your child, "If y is equal to 4 what is … $y + y$, $3 + y$, $y * 2$ and so on.
Unit 11	◆ Find two real world 3-dimensional shapes and guess which will have the greatest and the least volumes. Then find the volume of each one and check to see if your guess was correct.
Unit 12	◆ Reinforce ratios with a deck of cards. Ask your child, "What is the ratio of 3s to the whole deck?" (4 to 52 or 1 to 13); "Jacks to Aces and Queens?" (4 to 8 or 1 to 2); "Hearts to the whole deck?" (14 to 52 or 7 to 26).
	◆ In a parking lot, select a row or section and count the number of cars parked in that section. Ask how many of those cars in that section are red. Have your child determine the ratio of red cars to the number of cars parked in that section.

Do-Anytime Activities for Grade 6

These activities are easy and fun to do with your child at home, and they will reinforce the skills and concepts your child is learning in school.

Unit 1	◆ Scan the paper or magazines for graphs, and discuss with your child whether the information presented seems accurate or intentionally misleading. Analyze and discuss the statistics with your child to make it more meaningful. ◆ Ask your child to draw squares with an area of 12 square inches, of 8 square inches, and of 20 square inches.
Unit 2	◆ Have your child mentally calculate a tip from a restaurant bill. For example, if the bill is $25 and you intend to tip 15%, have your child go through the following mental algorithm: 10% of $25 is $2.50. Half of $2.50 (5%) is $1.25. $2.50 (10%) + $1.25 (5%) would be a tip of $3.75 (15%). The total amount to pay would be $28.75. ◆ Look through the paper for examples of number-and-word notation such as 7.5 million or 1.5 trillion, and ask your child to write the number in standard notation (7,500,000 or 1,500,000,000). If you can't find examples in the paper, make up some of your own.
Unit 3	◆ Create algebraic expressions that contain at least one variable. For example, you might say "John is 4 inches taller than his brother Sam." Ask your child to write the algebraic sentence which represents John's height ($S + 4$). Use family examples to make the expressions more meaningful. ◆ Name some fractions, decimals, or whole numbers, and have your child find the reciprocal of each. Remind your child to think "What times the number equals 1?" Try 4 ($\frac{1}{4}$), 0.3 ($\frac{10}{3}$), and $1\frac{1}{3}$ ($\frac{3}{4}$).
Unit 4	◆ When cooking in large quantities, ask your child to double or triple the amounts in your recipes. Watch to make sure that your child does the math for every ingredient. Or, halve a recipe if you need to make a smaller amount.
Unit 5	◆ Ask your child to find examples of right angles (90°), acute angles (less than 90°), and obtuse angles (between 90° and 180°). Guide your child to look particularly at bridge supports for a variety of angles. ◆ While driving in the car together, direct your child to look for congruent figures (two or more figures with the same size and shape). Windows in office buildings, circles on stop lights, and so on, can all represent congruent figures.

Unit 6	◆ Draw a number line from -5 to 5 with sidewalk chalk outside. Give your child addition or subtraction problems with positive and negative numbers. Have your child solve the problems by walking to the numbers while explaining his or her thinking.
	◆ Make up true and false number sentences. Ask your child to tell you whether each one is true or false and explain why. For example, try $30 * (4 - 2) > 60$ (false, because the answer is exactly 60) and $\frac{36}{4} * \frac{4}{2} = 18$ (true, because they equal each other). Switch roles.
Unit 7	◆ While playing a game that uses a die, keep a tally sheet of the total number of times you roll the die and how many times a certain number is rolled. For example, find how many times during the game that the number 5 comes up. Have your child write the probability for the chosen number. The probability is the number of times the chosen number came up over the number of times the die was rolled during the game. The probability will be close to $\frac{1}{6}$.
	◆ Try with your child to identify events that occur without dependence on any other event. Guide your child to see the different between *dependent* events and *random* events. For example, "Will Uncle Mike come for dinner?" depends on whether or not he got his car fixed. However, "Will I get HEADS when I flip this coin?" depends on no other event.
Unit 8	◆ Use graph paper to practice drawing shapes that are similar (exact shape but different size).
	◆ Encourage your child to read nutrition labels. Have him or her calculate the percent of fat in an item. $$\frac{\text{fat calories}}{\text{total calories}} = \frac{\text{percent of fat}}{100\%}$$ Your child should use cross-multiplication to solve the problem.
Unit 9	◆ Using a ruler to draw a rectangle, a triangle, and a parallelogram. With your child, recall the formula for finding the area of each shape: rectangle ($A = l * w$), triangle ($A = \frac{1}{2}b * h$), and parallelogram ($A = b * h$). Find the area of each shape in square inches.
	◆ Use graph paper to draw polygons with given areas. For example, see if your child can draw a trapezoid with an area of 20.5 square inches or a rectangle with an area of 30 square inches and a perimeter of 15 square inches.
Unit 10	◆ Review tessellations with your child. Encourage your child to name the *regular* tessellations and to draw and name the eight *semiregular* tessellations. Challenge your child to create *nonpolygonal Escher-type translation* tessellations. You may want to go to the library first and show your child examples of Escher's work.

Literature List for Grades 4–6

Your child will enjoy reading literature related to mathematics at home. Many of these titles can be found at your local library.

Number and Order

1, 2, 3, Go!
Huy Voun Lee
Henry Holt and Co., 2001

12 Ways to Get to 11
Eve Merriam
Aladdin Paperbacks, 1996

Can You Count to a Googol?
Robert E. Wells
Albert Whitman & Co., 2000

Count Your Way Through… series
James Haskins
Carolrhoda Books, 1987–1996

Counting on Frank
Rod Clement
Houghton Mifflin, 1994

fractals, googols, and other mathematical tales
Theoni Pappas
Wide World Publishing, 1993

Funny and Fabulous Fraction Stories
Dan Greenberg
Scholastic, 1999

G Is for Googol: A Math Alphabet Book
David Schwartz
Tricycle Press, 1998

The History of Counting
Denise Schmandt-Besserat
HarperCollins, 1999

How Much, How Many, How Far, How Heavy, How Long, How Tall is 1,000?
Helen Nolan
Kids Can Press, 2001

How Much Is a Million?
David Schwartz
HarperTrophy, 1993

Math Curse
Jon Sciezka
Puffin, 2004

Math Talk: Mathematical Ideas in Poems for Two Voices
Theoni Pappas
Wide World Publishing, 1991

Math-terpieces
Greg Tang
Scholastic, 2003

My Full Moon Is Square
Esther Pinczes
Houghton Mifflin, 2002

On Beyond a Million: An Amazing Math Journey
David Schwartz
Dragonfly, 2001

Sea Squares
Joy N. Hulme
Hyperion, 1993

Addition, Subtraction, Multiplication, and Division

The Amazing Pop-Up Multiplication Book
Kate Petty
Dutton, 1998

Anno's Mysterious Multiplying Jar
Mitsumasa and Masaichiro Anno
HarperTrophy, 1986

Arithme-Tickle: An Even Number of Odd Riddle-Rhymes
J. Patrick Lewis
Harcourt, 2002

The Best of Times
Greg Tang
Scholastic, 2002

The Grapes of Math
Greg Tang
Scholastic, 2001

The Great Divide:
    A Mathematical Marathon
Dayle Ann Dodds
Candlewick, 2005

A Remainder of One
Elinor Pinczes
Houghton Mifflin, 2002

Spaghetti and Meatballs for All
Marilyn Burns
Scholastic, 1999

Fractions, Decimals, and Percents; Rates and Proportions

Fraction Action
Loreen Leedy
Holiday House, 1996

Fraction Fun
David Adler
Holiday House, 1996

If Dogs Were Dinosaurs
David Schwartz
Scholastic, 2005

If You Hopped Like a Frog
David Schwartz
Scholastic, 1999

Piece=Part=Portion:
    Fractions=Decimals=Percents
Scott Gifford
Triangle Press, 2003

Data, Chance, and Probability

Do You Wanna Bet?
Jean Cushman
Clarion, 1991

How to Lie with Statistics
Darrell Huff
W.W. Norton, 1993

In the Next Three Seconds
Rowland Morgan
Puffin Books, 1999

Probably Pistachio
Stuart J. Murphy
HarperTrophy, 2001

Tiger Math: Learning to Graph
    from a Baby Tiger
Anne W. Nagda
Owlet Paperbacks, 2002

The Top 10 of Everything 2006
Russell Ash
DK Publishing, 2005

Geometry

The Art of Shapes for Children
    and Adults
Margaret Steele and Cindy Estes
Moca Store, 1997

A Cloak for the Dreamer
Arlene Friedman
Scholastic, 1995

The Dot and the Line: A Romance
    in Lower Mathematics
Norton Juster
Seastar, 2000

Geometric Patterns and
    How to Create Them
Clarence P. Hornung
Dover, 2001

Grandfather Tang's Story
Ann Tompert
Crown Publishers, 1990

*The Librarian Who
    Measured the Earth*
Kathryn Lasky
Little, Brown, 1994

*Mummy Math:
    An Adventure in Geometry*
Cindy Neuschwander
Henry Holt and Co., 2005

*Pigs on the Ball:
    Fun with Math & Sports*
Amy Axelrod
Aladdin, 2000

Shape Up!
David Adler
Holiday House, 2000

*Sir Cumference and the
    Dragon of Pi*
Cindy Neuschwander
Charlesbridge, 1999

*Sir Cumference and the
    Great Knight of Angleland*
Cindy Neuschwander
Charlesbridge, 2001

*Sir Cumference and the
    Sword in the Cone*
Cindy Neuschwander
Charlesbridge, 2003

The Tangram Book
Jerry Slocum
Sterling, 2003

What's Your Angle, Pythagoras?
Julie Ellis
Charlesbridge, 2004

Measurement

Actual Size
Steve Jenkins
Houghton Mifflin, 2004

*Fannie in the Kitchen: The Whole
    Story from Soup to Nuts of How
    Fannie Farmer Invented Recipes*
Deborah Hopkinson
Atheneum, 2001

Incredible Comparisons
Russell Ash
Dorling Kindersley, 1996

*Is a Blue Whale the Biggest
    Thing There Is?*
Robert E. Wells
Albert Whitman and Co., 1993

Measuring Weight and Time
Andrew King
Copper Beach, 1998

Reference Frames

A Fly on the Ceiling: A Math Myth
Julie Glass
Random House, 1998

Follow the Money
Loreen Leedy
Holiday House, Inc., 2003

*The Kids' Money Book:
    Earning, Saving, Spending,
    Investing, Donating*
Jamie Kyle McGillian
Sterling, 2003

Sea Clocks: The Story of Longitude
Louise Borden
Margaret K. McElderry Books,
    2004

*What's Faster Than a
    Speeding Cheetah?*
Robert E. Wells
Albert Whitman and Co., 1997

Patterns and Algebra Concepts

Anno's Magic Seeds
Mitsumasa Anno
Putnam Juvenile, 1999

Eight Hands Round:
    A Patchwork Alphabet
Ann Whitford Paul
HarperTrophy, 1998

A Grain of Rice
Helena Claire Pittman
Yearling, 1995

One Grain of Rice:
    A Mathematical Folktale
Demi
Scholastic, 1997

The Token Gift
Hugh William McKibbon
Annick, 1996

Problem Solving and Other Topics

25 Mini Math Mysteries
William Johnson
Scholastic, 1999

Albert Einstein: A Life of Genius
Elizabeth MacLeod
Kids Can Press, 2003

Career Ideas for Kids
    Who Like Math
Diane Lindsey Reeves
Checkmark Books, 2000

Computer Animation:
    From Start to Finish
Samuel G. Woods
Blackbirch, 2000

Count Down: Six Kids Vie for
    Glory at the World Toughest
    Math Competition
Steve Olson
Houghton Mifflin, 2004

Logic Puzzles to Bend Your Brain
Kurt Smith
Sterling, 2001

Math Stuff
Theoni Pappas
Wide World Publishing, 2002

Math Trek:
    Adventures in the Math Zone
Ivars Peterson
Jossey-Bass, 1999

Optical Illusion Magic: Visual
    Tricks and Amusements
Michael Anthony DiSpezio
Sterling, 2001

Real-World Math for
    Hands-On Fun!
Cindy Littlefield
Williamson Publishing, 2001

Commercial Games that Use Mathematics

Many games you have at home or see at the local store involve mathematical thinking. Students develop their skills in an almost effortless way when they play these games with each other and adults. The ages shown are suggested by the manufacturer, however, let the interest and motivation of your child be your guide when selecting and playing the games.

Counting, Adding, and Subtracting

Chutes and Ladders® (3+)

Hi Ho! Cherry-O® (3+)

Sorry!® (6+)

Trouble® (5+)

Uno® (6+)

Attributes, Patterns, and Geometry

Crazy Eights—traditional card game (4+)

Guess Who?® (6+)

Guess Where?® (6+)

jigsaw puzzles

Rummikub® (8+)

tangrams (5+)

Strategy and Spacial Perception

The a-MAZE-ing Labyrinth® (8+)

Battleship® (7+)

checkers (3+)

Clue® Jr. (5+) and Clue® (8+)

Connect Four® (7+)

Jenga® (6+)

mancala (6+)

memory (many names exist for this game of matching face-down pictures) (3+)

Mille Bornes® (8+)

Othello® (8+)

Pretty Pretty Princess® (5+)

More excellent games can be found on the Internet by searching under "educational math games."

Family Math Night: Planner

This worksheet will help you think through your Family Math Night in detail. Keeping the purpose and target participants in mind will help you select appropriate activities. Be sure to use this form with the Family Math Night: Activity Menu on the next page for more comprehensive planning.

Some helpful suggestions

♦ More families are generally able to attend events in the evening, but respect after-work time together by limiting events to 90 minutes or less.

♦ The sample schedules on pages 62 and 63 show typical Family Math Night agendas.

♦ Family events are effective when the activities are varied and interactive. Rotating stations assure that families can experience or learn several aspects of *Everyday Mathematics*.

After you complete the planner, it can help you compose an invitation to families.

Calendar	Date:		Time:	
Scope of event	School wide		Several classrooms	One classroom
Participants	Adults only		Adults & students	Whole family
Purpose	Program overview		Focus on games	Focus on a strand
	Focus on algorithms		Focus on routines	Other
Responsibilities	Coordinator: Additional support: Clean-up:			
Event Activities (Select from Family Math Night: Activity Menu, pp. 60 and 61.)	♦ Welcome—*teacher* ♦ _____ ♦ _____		♦ _____ ♦ _____ ♦ _____	
Take-Home Goodies	Information	Games or practice materials		Other
Follow-up/Evaluation	Written (p. 65)	Debrief with colleagues		Self-reflection

Family Math Night: Activity Menu

A successful event has three parts—introduction, main features, and wrap-up. This menu can help you choose the activities that will make up each part of your event. Before you begin, you may want to consider whether your event will cover numerous strands or focus just on one strand (such as algebra).

Introduction

Start off with a routine familiar to students, followed by information that will enhance families' understanding of the program.

- ◆ **Warm-Up** (whole group)
  - ☐ Name-collection boxes
  - ☐ Frames and Arrows
  - ☐ "What's My Rule?"
  - ☐ Math Message

- ◆ **Information** (whole group)
  - ☐ Program philosophy (p. 15)
  - ☐ Explanation of routines (pp. 23–26)
  - ☐ Examples of student work
  - ☐ How to help at home (pp. 46 and 47)

Main Features

Choose from several of the following activities to get participants actively involved. Consider having students lead as much as possible.

- ◆ **Activity Stations** (small groups or pairs)
  - ☐ Games
  - ☐ Algorithms and basic facts
  - ☐ Routines in *Everyday Mathematics*
  - ☐ Explorations and Projects
  - ☐ Math Boxes
  - ☐ Games on computer

- ◆ **Displays** (classrooms and hallways)
  - ☐ Photos (students doing activities, students and their products)
  - ☐ Products (charts, graphs, alternative algorithms, geometry constructions, written explanations)
  - ☐ Teacher-made charts about the program, such as a strand trace across grades

- ♦ **Literature Share** (whole group or small groups)
  - ☐ Mathematics-related literature book and short activity (teacher, student, or family member reads book aloud to model)

- ♦ **Make and Take** (small groups or pairs)
  - ☐ Fact Triangles
  - ☐ Game kits
  - ☐ Playing cards (Remark store-bought set; see the *Teacher's Reference Manual* for directions.)

Wrap-Up

Before you thank participants and ask for their feedback on the event, briefly discuss any lingering questions or comments. Consider using take-home goodies as a reward for turning in the evaluation.

- ♦ **Question and Answer Period** (free exchange between teacher and group)
- ♦ **Evaluation** (form on p. 65)
- ♦ **Take-Home Goodies**
  - ☐ Family Letter from current unit
  - ☐ Helpful lists from this handbook (Do-Anytime Activities, pp. 48–53, Literature Lists, pp. 54–57, and Commercial Games, p. 58)
  - ☐ Deck of playing cards (remarked) or Everything Math Deck
  - ☐ Fact Triangles
  - ☐ Ruler
  - ☐ Booklet of math games easily played at home (see *Teacher's Guide to Games*)

Family Math Night: Sample Schedule

Beginning of the Year (90 minutes)

Time	Activity	Materials
	Welcome	Name tags Juice or coffee
10 minutes	Introductions Purpose of Family Math Night Warm-up Activity: Estimation *How many pennies are in this jar?* Partners talk and write an estimate. Save estimates for Wrap-up.	Jar of small objects Index cards for family members to jot down estimates
5–10 minutes	Share letter from Superintendent or Board introducing strengths of program.* Explain philosophy and features of program.	Customized Parent Handbook, p. 8 *Everyday Mathematics* in the Classroom, p. 15 and Presenter's Notes, p. 16
10 minutes	Give overview of year and share the content emphasized in the program. Show and describe books, journals, tools.	Content Emphasized in *Everyday Mathematics*, pp. 19–21 Samples of materials
5 minutes	Explain role of games in program.	
15 minutes	Play game #1. Discuss math skills used, strategies, learning conversations.	Game-specific materials, copy of rules
15 minutes	Play game #2. Discuss math skills used, strategies, learning conversations.	Game-specific materials, copy of rules
10 minutes	Briefly review your customized Parent Handbook. Describe your home communication.	Parent Handbook
10 minutes	Wrap-up: Volunteers share their estimates and estimating strategies from the Warm-up Activity. Point out that the program asks students to explain their thinking in a similar way.	
5 minutes	Evaluation/questionnaire	Copies of evaluation

* For program users in first year

Family Math Night: Sample Schedule

Middle of the Year (90 minutes)

Time	Activity	Materials
10 minutes	Welcome Introductions Purpose of the Family Math Night	Name tags
15 minutes	Overview of units and projects completed so far View students' portfolios.	Students' portfolios
5 minutes	Orientation to stations and questions for parents to ask their children	Handout (optional)
10 minutes each = 50 minutes total (allows time for changing stations)	4 Stations—one led by teacher, others led by students Rotate among: • Program Topic [for example, *What is an algorithm?*] (led by teacher) • Game #1 • Display of Projects or Explorations • Game #2 or Technology Time	Materials specific to station activities
10 minutes	Wrap-up: Comments, questions Congratulations to students	Take-home goodies

Family Math Night: Sample Invitation

Dear Families,

The beginning of the school year has been fun and exciting! I look forward to working with your children this year.

One of our favorite parts of the school day has been the time we spend on our math program, *Everyday Mathematics*. To have a clear idea of what is being taught in math this year, how it is being taught, and how you can support your child at home, we are holding a **Family Math Night** on **Tuesday, September 22**, from **7:00 P.M.** to **8:30 P.M.**

Please come to this fun and informative event to learn about *Everyday Mathematics* and receive your own Parent Handbook. I hope that at least one family member will attend for each student. **Please fill out the attached tear-off form and return it by Friday, September 18** so I can have enough materials ready for all who attend. I look forward to seeing you there!

Sincerely,

- -

Family Math Night   Date: _____   Time: _____

Student's name _____

☐ Yes, I/we will attend Family Math Night on Tuesday, September 22.

    Number of people_____

    Names attending _____

☐ No, I am unable to attend, but please send me the Parent Handbook.

Family Math Night: Evaluation

Thank you for coming to this event! Please take a few minutes to answer the following questions. I will use your feedback to improve my communications with you and make the next Family Math Night an even bigger success. Thank you again.

Please respond to these statements using a scale of 1 (strongly disagree) to 5 (strongly agree). Feel free to write comments as well.

Family Math Night was fun and worthwhile.   1   2   3   4   5

I learned a great deal about the
mathematics my child is learning.   1   2   3   4   5

My questions about *Everyday Mathematics*
were answered.   1   2   3   4   5

I feel more knowledgeable about how to
help my child with math at home.   1   2   3   4   5

I would like to attend another math event.   1   2   3   4   5

Please write your answers to these questions below. (Use the back of this page if you need more space.)

What would you like to hear about, see, or do at the next Family Math Night?

_____

_____

What would make it easier for you to help your child with math at home?

_____

_____

Please write any questions you may have that were not answered.

_____

_____

Which of the following *Everyday Mathematics* activities would you like to help with in the classroom?

☐ Projects   ☐ Guest Speaker (how you use math in your job)

☐ Preparing materials   ☐ Other suggestions

☐ Games

Portfolio Reflection

To prepare your portfolio, put all of your work in order with the oldest work on top and the most recent work on the bottom.

Look through your work again. Think about which piece represents your best work, your most challenging work, your best work with a partner or group, and the work you would most like to improve.

Cut out the cards. Finish the sentences and then attach the cards to the appropriate piece.

✂

Best Thinking

This piece of work shows my best thinking because _____

_____

_____

_____

_____

_____

_____

Most Challenging

This piece of work was the most challenging for me because _____

_____

_____

_____

_____

_____

_____

Best Cooperative Work

This piece of work shows my best work with others because _____

_____

_____

_____

_____

_____

_____

Needs Improvement

I would like to improve this piece of work because _____

_____

_____

_____

_____

_____

_____

Game Feedback

Your name: _____ Student's name: _____

Which game did you play? _____

How much time did you spend playing? _____

Was this game fun? _____

What skills do you think your child learned or strengthened while playing the game?

_____

_____

How would you rate this game for your child?

1	2	3	4	5
(too easy)		(just right)		(too difficult)

- -

Observation Request

Your name: _____ Student's name: _____

I would like to observe my child's mathematics lesson.

I am available on these dates:

1) _____, _____   2) _____, _____
      (day)   (date)   (day)   (date)

I am most interested in seeing and learning about_____

_____

I understand that you will let me know which date works best for you and the class.

Please contact me by: ☐ letter ☐ phone _____ ☐ e-mail_____

Volunteers Welcome!

Help strengthen our mathematics program and find out what your child is learning by volunteering your time.

Which of the following *Everyday Mathematics* activities would you like to help with?

☐ Games (play skill-building games with students; 30 minutes)

☐ Projects (supervise and guide students; 1 hour)

☐ Preparing materials (get items ready for activities; 1 hour—can be after school)

☐ Planning/helping with family events (many ways to help—commitment time varies)

Name: _____   Student's name: _____

Phone: _____   Best time to contact: _____

✂ -

Thank You for Volunteering!

Dear _____,

You offered to help with the following activity: _____

Here are some dates and times when we are in need of volunteer help:

Choice 1: _____, _____

Choice 2: _____, _____

Please let me know which of these times you are available.

Thank you very much!

Sincerely,

_____

phone/e-mail: _____

Classroom Helper Feedback

Thank you for helping with math today! Here is some information you need to assist with today's activities.

Classroom Helper: _____ Date: _____

Activity: _____

Where to find directions and materials: _____

Students to work with: _____ _____

_____ _____

Goals: _____

_____

_____

_____

- -

Before you leave, please write a few notes describing how everything went, and check in with the teacher.

Thank you!

Classroom Helper's Notes

_____

_____

_____

_____

_____

_____

absolute value The distance between a number and 0 on the number line. The absolute value of a positive number is the number itself. The absolute value of a negative number is the opposite of the number. For example, the absolute value of 3 is 3, and the absolute value of -6 is 6. The absolute value of 0 is 0. The notation for the absolute value of a number n is $|n|$.

addend Any one of a set of numbers that are added. For example, in $5 + 3 + 1 = 9$, the addends are 5, 3, and 1.

adjacent angles Angles that are next to each other; adjacent angles have a common vertex and common side but no other overlap.

algebraic expression An expression that contains a variable. For example, if Maria is 2 inches taller than Joe and if the variable M represents Maria's height, then the algebraic expression $M - 2$ represents Joe's height.

algorithm A set of step-by-step instructions for doing something, such as carrying out a computation or solving a problem.

angle A figure that is formed by two rays or two line segments with a common endpoint. The rays or segments are called the *sides* of the angle. The common endpoint is called the *vertex* of the angle. Angles are measured in *degrees* (°). An *acute angle* has a measure greater than 0° and less than 90°. An *obtuse angle* has a measure greater than 90° and less than 180°. A *reflex angle* has a measure greater than

180° and less than 360°. A *right angle* measures 90°. A *straight angle* measures 180°.

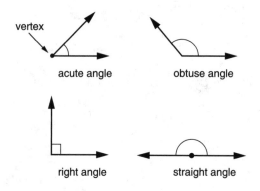

arc Part of a circle, from one point on the circle to another. For example, a semicircle is an arc whose endpoints are the endpoints of a diameter of the circle.

area The amount of surface inside a closed boundary. Area is measured in square units, such as square inches or square centimeters.

area model (1) A model for multiplication problems in which the length and width of a rectangle represent the factors, and the area of the rectangle represents the product. (2) A model for showing fractions as parts of circles, rectangles, or other geometric figures.

array (1) An arrangement of objects in a regular pattern, usually in rows and columns. (2) A rectangular array. In *Everyday Mathematics*, an array is a rectangular array unless otherwise specified.

Associative Property A property of addition and multiplication (but not of subtraction or division) that says that when you add or multiply three

numbers, it does not matter which two you add or multiply first. For example:
$$(4 + 3) + 7 = 4 + (3 + 7) \text{ and}$$
$$(5 * 8) * 9 = 5 * (8 * 9).$$

average A typical value for a set of numbers. The word *average* usually refers to the *mean* of a set of numbers.

axis (plural: **axes**) (1) Either of the two number lines that intersect to form a coordinate grid. (2) A line about which a solid figure rotates.

base (in exponential notation) The number that is raised to a power. For example, in 5^3, the base is 5. See also *exponential notation* and *power of a number*.

base-ten Our system for writing numbers that uses only 10 symbols, called *digits*. The digits are 0, 1, 2, 3, 4, 5, 6, 7, 8, and 9. You can write any number using only these 10 digits. Each digit has a value that depends on its place in the number. In this system, moving a digit one place to the left makes that digit worth 10 times as much. And moving a digit one place to the right makes that digit worth one-tenth as much. See also *place value*.

bisect To divide a segment, an angle, or another figure into two equal parts.

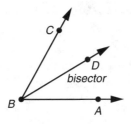

Ray *BD* bisects angle *ABC*.

change diagram A diagram used in *Everyday Mathematics* to represent situations in which quantities are increased or decreased.

circle graph A graph in which a circle and its interior are divided by radii into parts (*sectors*) to show the parts of a set of data. The whole circle represents the whole set of data. Same as *pie graph*.

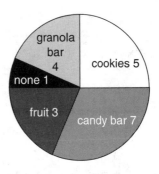

circumference The distance around a circle; the perimeter of a circle.

column-addition method A method for adding numbers in which the addends' digits are first added in each place-value column separately, and then 10-for-1 trades are made until each column has only one digit. Lines are drawn to separate the place-value columns.

column-division method A division procedure in which vertical lines are drawn between the digits of the dividend. As needed, trades are made from one column into the next column at the right. The lines make the procedure easier to carry out.

common denominator (1) If two fractions have the same denominator, that denominator is called a common denominator. (2) For two or more fractions, any number that is a *common multiple* of their denominators. For example, the fractions $\frac{1}{2}$ and $\frac{2}{3}$ have the common denominators 6, 12, 18, and so on. See also *quick common denominator*.

common factor A counting number is a common factor of two or more counting numbers if it is a *factor* of each of those numbers. For example, 4 is a common factor of 8 and 12. See also *factor of a counting number* n.

common multiple A number is a common multiple of two or more numbers if it is a *multiple* of each of those numbers. The multiples of 2 are 2, 4, 6, 8, 10, 12, and so on; the multiples of 3 are 3, 6, 9, 12, and so on; and the common multiples of 2 and 3 are 6, 12, 18 and so on.

Commutative Property A property of addition and multiplication (but not of subtraction or division) that says that changing the order of the numbers being added or multiplied does not change the answer. These properties are often called *turn-around facts* in *Everyday Mathematics*. For example: 5 + 10 = 10 + 5 and 3 * 8 = 8 * 3.

comparison diagram A diagram used in *Everyday Mathematics* to represent situations in which two quantities are compared.

complementary angles Two angles whose measures total 90°.

concave polygon A polygon in which at least one vertex is "pushed in." At least one inside angle of a concave polygon is a reflex angle (has a measure greater than 180°). Same as *nonconvex polygon*.

concentric circles Circles that have the same center but radii of different lengths.

congruent Having the same shape and size. Two 2-dimensional figures are congruent if they match exactly when one is placed on top of the other. (It may be necessary to flip one of the figures over.)

consecutive angles Two angles in a polygon that share a common side.

convex polygon A polygon in which all vertices are "pushed outward." Each inside angle of a convex polygon has a measure less than 180°.

corresponding Having the same relative position in *similar* or *congruent* figures. In the diagram, pairs of

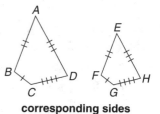

corresponding sides

corresponding sides are marked with the same number of slash marks and *corresponding angles* are marked with the same number of arcs.

counting numbers The numbers used to count things. The set of counting numbers is {1, 2, 3, 4, ...}. Compare to *whole numbers*.

cross multiplication The process of finding the cross products of a *proportion*. Cross multiplication can be used in solving proportions.

cubic unit A unit used in measuring volume, such as a cubic centimeter or a cubic foot.

degree (°) (1) A unit of measure for angles based on dividing a circle into 360 equal parts. Latitude and longitude are measured in degrees, and these degrees are based on angle measures. (2) A unit of measure for temperature. In all cases, a small raised circle (°) is used to show degrees.

denominator The number below the line in a fraction. A fraction may be used to name part of a whole. If the *whole* (the *ONE*, or the *unit*) is divided into equal parts, the denominator represents the number of equal parts into which the whole is divided. In the fraction $\frac{a}{b}$, b is the denominator.

density A *rate* that compares the weight of an object with its *volume*. For example, suppose a ball has a weight of 20 grams and a volume of 10 cubic centimeters. To find its density, divide its weight by its volume: 20 g / 10 cm³ = 2 g / cm³, or 2 grams per cubic centimeter.

diameter (1) A line segment that passes through the center of a circle or sphere and has endpoints on the circle or sphere. (2) The length of this line segment. The diameter of a circle or sphere is twice the length of its *radius*.

difference The result of subtracting one number from another. See also *minuend* and *subtrahend*.

digit One of the number symbols 0, 1, 2, 3, 4, 5, 6, 7, 8, and 9 in the standard, *base-ten* system.

Distributive Property A property that relates multiplication and addition or subtraction. This property gets its name because it "distributes" a factor over terms inside parentheses.
Distributive property of multiplication over addition:
$a * (b + c) = (a * b) + (a * c)$,
so $2 * (5 + 3) = (2 * 5) + (2 * 3)$
$= 10 + 6 = 16$.
Distributive property of multiplication over subtraction:
$a * (b - c) = (a * b) - (a * c)$,
so $2 * (5 - 3) = (2 * 5) - (2 * 3)$
$= 10 - 6 = 4$.

dividend The number in division that is being divided. For example, in $35 \div 5 = 7$, the dividend is 35.

divisibility test A test to find out whether one counting number is *divisible by* another counting number without actually doing the division. A divisibility test for 5, for example, is to check the digit in the 1s place: if that digit is 0 or 5, then the number is divisible by 5.

divisible by If one counting number can be divided by a second counting number with a remainder of 0, then the first number is divisible by the second number. For example, 28 is divisible by 7 because 28 divided by 7 is 4, with a remainder of 0.

Division of Fractions Property A fact that makes division with fractions easier: division by a fraction is the same as multiplication by that fraction's *reciprocal*. For example, because the reciprocal of $\frac{1}{2}$ is 2, the division problem $4 \div \frac{1}{2}$ is equivalent to the multiplication problem $4 * 2$. See also *multiplicative inverses*.

divisor In division, the number that divides another number. For example, in $35 \div 5 = 7$, the divisor is 5.

edge A line segment or curve where two surfaces meet.

equation A number sentence that contains an equal sign. For example, $15 = 10 + 5$ is an equation.

equivalent equations Equations that have the same *solution set*. For example, $2 + x = 4$ and $6 + x = 8$ are equivalent equations because the solution set for each is $x = 2$.

equivalent fractions Fractions with different denominators that name the same number. For example, $\frac{1}{2}$ and $\frac{4}{8}$ are equivalent fractions.

equivalent rates *Rates* that make the same comparison. For example, the rates $\frac{60 \text{ miles}}{1 \text{ hour}}$ and $\frac{1 \text{ mile}}{1 \text{ minute}}$ are equivalent. Two rates named as fractions using the *same units* are equivalent if the fractions (ignoring the units) are equivalent. For example, $\frac{12 \text{ pages}}{4 \text{ minutes}}$ and $\frac{6 \text{ pages}}{2 \text{ minutes}}$ are equivalent rates because $\frac{12}{4}$ and $\frac{6}{2}$ are equivalent.

equivalent ratios *Ratios* that make the same comparison. Two or more ratios are equivalent if they can be named as equivalent fractions. For example, the ratios 12 to 20, 6 to 10, and 3 to 5 are equivalent ratios because $\frac{12}{20} = \frac{6}{10} = \frac{3}{5}$.

exponent A small raised number used in *exponential notation* to tell how many times the *base* is used as a *factor*. For example, in 5^3, the base is 5, the exponent is 3, and $5^3 = 5 * 5 * 5 = 125$. See also *power of a number*.

exponential notation A way to show repeated multiplication by the same factor. For example, 2^3 is exponential notation for $2 * 2 * 2$. The small raised 3 is the *exponent*. It tells how many times the number 2, called the *base*, is used as a factor.

extended multiplication fact A multiplication fact involving multiples of 10, 100, and so on. For example, $6 * 70$, $60 * 7$, and $60 * 70$ are extended multiplication facts.

face A flat surface on a 3-dimensional shape.

fact family A set of related addition and subtraction facts, or related multiplication and division facts. For example, $5 + 6 = 11$, $6 + 5 = 11$, $11 - 5 = 6$, and $11 - 6 = 5$ are a fact family. $5 * 7 = 35$, $7 * 5 = 35$, $35 \div 5 = 7$, and $35 \div 7 = 5$ are another fact family.

factor (in a product) Whenever two or more numbers are multiplied to give a product, each of the numbers that is multiplied is called a factor. For example, in $4 * 1.5 = 6$, 6 is the product and 4 and 1.5 are called factors. See also *factor of a counting number* n. **Note:** This definition of *factor* is much less important than the definition below.

factor of a counting number *n* A counting number whose product with some other counting number equals *n*. For example, 2 and 3 are factors of 6 because $2 * 3 = 6$. But 4 is not a factor of 6 because $4 * 1.5 = 6$ and 1.5 is not a counting number.

$$2 * 3 = 6$$
$$\uparrow \ \uparrow \qquad \uparrow$$
$$\text{factors} \quad \text{product}$$

Note: This definition of *factor* is much more important than the previous definition.

factor pair Two factors of a counting number whose product is the number. A number may have more than one factor pair. For example, the factor pairs for 18 are 1 and 18, 2 and 9, and 3 and 6.

factor rainbow A way to show factor pairs in a list of all the factors of a counting number. A factor rainbow can be used to check whether a list of factors is correct.

factor string A counting number written as a product of two or more of its factors. The number 1 is never part of a factor string. For example, a factor string for 24 is $2 * 3 * 4$. This factor string has three factors, so its length is 3. Another factor string for 24 is $2 * 3 * 2 * 2$ (length 4).

factor tree A way to get the *prime factorization* of a counting number. Write the original number as a product of counting-number factors. Then write each of these factors as a product of factors, and so on, until the factors are all prime numbers. A factor tree looks like an upside-down tree, with the root (the original number) at the top and the leaves (the factors) beneath it.

```
    30
   /\
  6 * 5
 /\  \
2 * 3 * 5
```

factorial A product of a whole number and all the smaller whole numbers except 0. An exclamation point (!) is used to write factorials. For example, "three factorial" is written as 3! and is equal to $3 * 2 * 1 = 6$. $10! = 10 * 9 * 8 * 7 * 6 * 5 * 4 * 3 * 2 * 1 = 3{,}628{,}800$. 0! is defined to be equal to 1.

figurate numbers Numbers that can be shown by specific geometric patterns. Square numbers and triangular numbers are examples of figurate numbers.

fraction A number in the form $\frac{a}{b}$ where a and b are whole numbers and b is not 0. A fraction may be used to name part of a whole, or to compare two quantities. A fraction may also be used to represent division. For example, $\frac{2}{3}$ can be thought of as 2 divided by 3. See also *numerator* and *denominator*.

Fraction-Stick Chart A diagram used in *Everyday Mathematics* to represent simple fractions.

Geometry Template An *Everyday Mathematics* tool that includes a millimeter ruler, a ruler with sixteenth-inch intervals, half-circle and full-circle protractors, a percent circle, pattern-block shapes, and other geometric figures. The template can also be used as a compass.

greatest common factor (GCF) The largest factor that two or more counting numbers have in common. For example, the common factors of 24 and 36 are 1, 2, 3, 4, 6, and 12. The greatest common factor of 24 and 36 is 12.

horizontal In a left-right orientation; parallel to the horizon.

hypotenuse In a right triangle, the side opposite the right angle.

image The reflection of an object that you see when you look in a mirror. Also, a figure that is produced by a *transformation* (a *reflection*, *translation*, or *rotation*, for example) of another figure. See also *preimage*.

improper fraction A fraction whose numerator is greater than or equal to its denominator. For example, $\frac{4}{3}, \frac{5}{2}, \frac{4}{4}$, and $\frac{24}{12}$ are improper fractions. In *Everyday Mathematics*, improper fractions are sometimes called "top-heavy" fractions.

indirect measurement Determining heights, distances, and other quantities that cannot be measured directly.

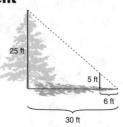

inequality A number sentence with $>$, $<$, $\geq$, $\leq$, or $\neq$. For example, the sentence $8 < 15$ is an inequality.

inscribed polygon A polygon whose vertices are all on the same circle.

integer A number in the set $\{\ldots, -4, -3, -2, -1, 0, 1, 2, 3, 4, \ldots\}$; a *whole* *number* or the opposite of a whole number, where 0 is its own opposite.

irrational number A number that cannot be written as a fraction, where both the numerator and the denominator are *integers* and the denominator is not zero. For example, π (pi) is an irrational number.

isometry transformation A transformation such as a *translation* (slide), *reflection* (flip), or *rotation* (turn) that changes the position or orientation of a figure but does not change its size or shape.

landmark A notable feature of a data set. Landmarks include the *median*, *mode*, *maximum*, *minimum*, and *range*. The *mean* can also be thought of as a landmark.

lattice method A very old way to multiply multidigit numbers.

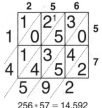

$256 * 57 = 14,592$

least common denominator (LCD) The *least common multiple* of the denominators of every fraction in a given collection. For example, the least common denominator of $\frac{1}{2}$, $\frac{4}{5}$, and $\frac{3}{8}$ is 40.

least common multiple (LCM) The smallest number that is a multiple of two or more numbers. For example, while some common multiples of 6 and 8 are 24, 48, and 72, the least common multiple of 6 and 8 is 24.

left-to-right subtraction A subtraction method in which you start at the left and subtract column by column.

like terms In an *algebraic expression*, either the constant terms or any terms that contain the same variable(s) raised to the same power(s). For example, $4y$ and $7y$ are like terms in the expression $4y + 7y - z$.

line graph A graph in which data points are connected by line segments.

line of reflection (mirror line) A line halfway between a figure (preimage) and its reflected image. In a *reflection*, a figure is "flipped over" the line of reflection.

line of symmetry A line drawn through a figure so that it is divided into two parts that are mirror images of each other. The two parts look alike but face in opposite directions.

line plot A sketch of data in which check marks, Xs, or other marks above a labeled line show the frequency of each value.

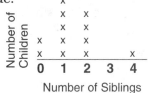

lowest terms See *simplest form*.

magnitude estimate A rough estimate. A magnitude estimate tells whether an answer should be in the tens, hundreds, thousands, ten thousands, and so on.

mean The sum of a set of numbers divided by the number of numbers in the set. The mean is often referred to simply as the *average*.

median The middle value in a set of data when the data are listed in order from smallest to largest, or from largest to smallest. If there are an even number of data points, the median is the *mean* of the two middle values.

minuend In subtraction, the number from which another number is subtracted. For example, in $19 - 5 = 14$, the minuend is 19. See also *subtrahend*.

mixed number A number that is written using both a whole number and a fraction. For example, $2\frac{1}{4}$ is a mixed number equal to $2 + \frac{1}{4}$.

mode The value or values that occur most often in a set of data.

multiple of a number n (1) A product of n and a counting number. For example, the multiples of 7 are 7, 14, 21, 28, ... (2) a product of n and an integer. The multiples of 7 are ..., -21, -14, -7, 0, 7, 14, 21, ...

multiplication diagram A diagram used for problems in which there are several equal groups. The diagram has three parts: a number of groups, a number in each group, and a total number. Also called *multiplication / division diagram*.

multiplication property of – 1 A property of multiplication that says that for any number a, $(-1) * a = \text{OPP}(a)$ or $-a$. For $a = 5$: $(-1) * 5 = \text{OPP}(5) = -5$. For $a = -3$: $(-1) * (-3) = \text{OPP}(-3) = -(-3) = 3$.

multiplicative inverses Two numbers whose product is 1. The multiplicative inverse of 5 is $\frac{1}{5}$, and the multiplicative inverse of $\frac{3}{5}$ is $\frac{5}{3}$. Multiplicative inverses are also called *reciprocals* of each other.

name-collection box A diagram that is used for writing equivalent names for a number.

negative number A number that is less than zero; a number to the left of zero on a horizontal number line or zero on a vertical number line. The symbol $-$ may be used to write a negative number. For example, "negative 5" is usually written as -5.

nonconvex polygon See *concave polygon*.

number-and-word notation A way of writing a number using a combination of numbers and words. For example, 27 billion is number-and-word notation for 27,000,000,000.

number sentence At least two numbers or expressions separated by a relation symbol ($=$, $>$, $<$, $\geq$, $\leq$, $\neq$). Most number sentences contain at least one *operation symbol* ($+$, $-$, $\times$, $*$, $\div$, $/$). Number sentences may also have grouping symbols, such as parentheses and brackets.

numerator The number above the line in a fraction. A fraction may be used to name part of a whole. If the *whole* (the *ONE*, or the *unit*) is divided into equal parts, the numerator represents the number of equal parts being considered. In the fraction $\frac{a}{b}$, a is the numerator.

ONE See *whole* and *unit*.

open sentence A *number sentence* which has *variables* in place of one or more missing numbers. An open sentence is usually neither true nor false. For example, $5 + x = 13$ is an open sentence. The sentence is true if 8 is substituted for x. The sentence is false if 4 is substituted for x.

operation symbol A symbol used to stand for a mathematical operation. Common operation symbols are $+$, $-$, $\times$, $*$, $\div$, and $/$.

opposite angles (1) of a quadrilateral: Angles that do not share a common side.

(2) of a triangle: An angle is opposite the side of a triangle that is not one of the sides of the angle. (3) of two lines that intersect: The angles that do not share a common side are opposite angles. Opposite angles have equal measures. Same as *vertical angles*.

order of operations Rules that tell in what order to perform operations in arithmetic and algebra. The order of operations is as follows:
1) Do the operations in parentheses first. (Use rules 2–4 inside the parentheses.)
2) Calculate all the expressions with exponents.
3) Multiply and divide in order from left to right.
4) Add and subtract in order from left to right.

ordered number pair (ordered pair) Two numbers that are used to locate a point on a *rectangular coordinate grid*. The first number gives the position along the horizontal axis, and the second number gives the position along the vertical axis. The numbers in an ordered pair are called coordinates. Ordered pairs are usually written inside parentheses: (5,3). See *rectangular coordinate grid* for an illustration.

origin (1) The 0 point on a number line. (2) The point (0,0) where the two axes of a coordinate grid meet.

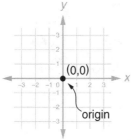

outcome A possible result of an experiment or situation. For example, HEADS and TAILS are the two possible outcomes of tossing a coin.

parallel Lines, line segments, or rays in the same plane are parallel if they never cross or meet, no matter how far they are extended. Two planes are parallel if they never cross or meet. A line and a plane are parallel if they never cross or meet. The symbol ‖ means *is parallel to*.

partial-differences method A way to subtract in which differences are computed for each place (ones, tens, hundreds, and so on) separately. The partial differences are then combined to give the final answer.

partial-products method A way to multiply in which the value of each digit in one factor is multiplied by the value of each digit in the other factor. The final product is the sum of these partial products.

partial-quotients method A way to divide in which the dividend is divided in a series of steps. The quotients for each step (called partial quotients) are added to give the final answer.

partial-sums method A way to add in which sums are computed for each place (ones, tens, hundreds, and so on) separately. The partial-sums are then added to give the final answer.

parts-and-total diagram A diagram used in *Everyday Mathematics* to represent situations in which two or more quantities are combined to form a total quantity.

part-to-part ratio A *ratio* that compares a part of a whole to another part of the same whole. For example, the statement "There are 8 boys for every 12 girls" expresses a part-to-part ratio. See also *part-to-whole ratio*.

part-to-whole ratio A *ratio* that compares a part of a whole to the whole. For example, the statements "8 out of 20 students are boys" and "12 out of 20 students are girls," both express part-to-whole ratios. See also *part-to-part ratio*.

percent (%) Per hundred or out of a hundred. For example, "48% of the students in the school are boys" means that 48 out of every 100 students in the school are boys; $48\% = \frac{48}{100} = 0.48$.

Percent Circle A tool on the *Geometry Template* that is used to measure and draw figures that involve percents (such as circle graphs).

perimeter The distance around a 2-dimensional shape, along the boundary of the shape. The perimeter of a circle is called its *circumference*. A formula for the perimeter P of a rectangle with length l and width w is $P = 2 * (l + w)$.

perpendicular Crossing or meeting at *right angles*. Lines, rays, line segments, or planes that cross or meet at right angles are perpendicular. The symbol, $\perp$, means is *perpendicular* to.

per-unit rate A *rate* with 1 in the denominator. Per-unit rates tell how many of one thing there are for one of another thing. For example, "2 dollars per gallon" is a per-unit rate. "12 miles per hour" and "4 words per minute" are also examples of per-unit rates.

pi (π) The ratio of the *circumference* of a circle to its *diameter*. Pi is also the ratio of the area of a circle to the square of its radius. Pi is the same for every circle and is an irrational number that is approximately equal to 3.14. Pi is the sixteenth letter of the Greek alphabet and is written π.

pie graph See *circle graph*.

place value A system that gives a digit a value according to its position in a number. In our *base-ten* system for writing numbers, moving a digit one place to the left makes that digit worth 10 times as much, and moving a digit one place to the right makes that digit worth one-tenth as much. For example, in the number 456, the 4 in the hundreds place is worth 400; but in the number 45.6, the 4 in the tens place is worth 40.

plane A flat surface that extends forever.

point symmetry A figure has point symmetry if it can be rotated 180° about a point in such a way that the resulting figure (the *image*) exactly matches the original figure (the *preimage*). Point symmetry is *rotation symmetry* in which the turn is 180°.

polygon A 2-dimensional figure that is made up of three or more line segments joined end to end to make one closed path. The line segments of a polygon may not cross.

polyhedron A geometric solid whose surfaces (*faces*) are all flat and formed by polygons. Each face consists of a polygon and the interior of that polygon. A polyhedron does not have any curved surfaces.

positive number A number that is greater than zero; a number to the right of zero on a horizontal number line, or above zero on a vertical number line. A positive number may be written using the + symbol, but is usually written without it. For example, $+10 = 10$ and $\pi = +\pi$.

power of a number The product of factors that are all the same. For example, $5 * 5 * 5$ (or 125) is called "5 to the third power" or "the third power of 5" because 5 is a factor three times. $5 * 5 * 5$ can also be written as 5^3. See also *exponent*.

power of 10 A whole number that can be written as a *product of 10s*. For example, 100 is equal to $10 * 10$, or 10^2. 100 is called "the second power of 10" or "10 to the second power." A number that can be written as a *product of* $\frac{1}{10s}$ is also a power of 10. For example, $10^{-2} = \frac{1}{10^2} = \frac{1}{10 * 10} = \frac{1}{10} * \frac{1}{10}$ is a power of 10.

preimage A geometric figure that is changed (by a *reflection*, *rotation*, or *translation*, for example) to produce another figure. See also *image*.

prime factorization A counting number expressed as a product of prime factors. Every counting number greater than 1 can be written as a product of prime factors in only one way. For example, the prime factorization of 24 is $2 * 2 * 2 * 3$. (The order of the factors does not matter; $2 * 3 * 2 * 2$ is also the prime factorization of 24.) The prime factorization of a prime number is that number. For example, the prime factorization of 13 is 13.

prime number A counting number that has exactly two different *factors*: itself and 1. For example, 5 is a prime number because its only factors are 5 and 1. The number 1 is not a prime number because that number has only a single factor, the number 1 itself.

probability A number from 0 through 1 that tells the chance that an event will happen. The closer a probability is to 1, the more likely the event is to happen.

product The result of multiplying two numbers, called *factors*. For example, in $4 * 3 = 12$, the product is 12.

proper factor Any *factor of a counting number* except the number itself. For example, the *factors* of 10 are 1, 2, 5, and 10, and the *proper factors* of 10 are 1, 2, and 5.

proper fraction A fraction in which the numerator is less than the denominator; a proper fraction names a number that is less than 1. For example, $\frac{3}{4}$, $\frac{2}{5}$, and $\frac{12}{24}$ are proper fractions.

proportion A number model that states that two fractions are equal. Often the fractions in a proportion represent rates or ratios.

protractor A tool on the *Geometry Template* that is used to measure and draw angles. The half-circle protractor can be used to measure and draw angles up to $180°$; the full-circle protractor, to measure angles up to $360°$.

Pythagorean Theorem The following famous *theorem*: If the *legs of a right triangle* have lengths a and b and the *hypotenuse* has length c, then $a^2 + b^2 = c^2$.

quick common denominator The product of the denominators of two or more fractions. For example, the quick common denominator of $\frac{1}{4}$ and $\frac{3}{6}$ is $4 * 6$, or 24. As the name suggests, this is a quick way to get a *common* *denominator* for a collection of fractions, but it does not necessarily give the *least common denominator*.

quotient The result of dividing one number by another number. For example, in $35 \div 5 = 7$, the quotient is 7.

radius (plural: **radii**) (1) A line segment from the center of a circle (or sphere) to any point on the circle (or sphere). (2) The length of this line segment.

random numbers Numbers produced by an experiment, such as rolling a die or spinning a spinner, in which all *outcomes* are equally likely. For example, rolling a fair die produces random numbers because each of the six possible numbers 1, 2, 3, 4, 5 and 6 has the same chance of coming up.

range The difference between the maximum and the minimum in a set of data.

rate A comparison by division of two quantities with *unlike units*. For example, a speed such as 55 miles per hour is a rate that compares distance with time. See also *ratio*.

ratio A comparison by division of two quantities with *like units*. Ratios can be expressed with fractions, decimals, percents, or words. Sometimes they are written with a colon between the two numbers that are being compared. For example, if a team wins 3 games out of 5 games played, the ratio of wins to total games can be written as $\frac{3}{5}$, 0.6, 60%, 3 to 5, or 3:5. See also *rate*.

rational number Any number that can be written or renamed as a *fraction* or the *opposite* of a fraction. Most of the numbers you have used are rational numbers. For example, $\frac{2}{3}$, $-\frac{2}{3}$, $60\% = \frac{60}{100}$, and $-1.25 = -\frac{5}{4}$ are all rational numbers.

ray A straight path that starts at one point (called the endpoint) and continues forever in one direction.

real number Any *rational* or *irrational* number.

reciprocal Same as *multiplicative inverse*.

rectangle method A method for finding area in which rectangles are drawn around a figure or parts of a figure. The rectangles form regions with boundaries that are rectangles or triangular halves of rectangles. The area of the original figure can be found by adding or subtracting the areas of these regions.

rectangular coordinate grid A device for locating points in a plane using *ordered number pairs*, or coordinates. A rectangular coordinate grid is formed by two number lines that intersect at their zero points and form right angles. Also called a coordinate grid.

reflection The "flipping" of a figure over a line (the *line of reflection*) so that its *image* is the mirror image of the original figure (*preimage*). A reflection of a solid figure is a mirror-image "flip" over a plane.

regular polygon A polygon whose sides are all the same length and whose interior angles are all equal.

regular polyhedron A polyhedron whose faces are congruent and formed by *regular polygons*, and whose vertices all look the same. There are five regular polyhedrons.

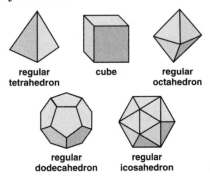

regular tetrahedron   cube   regular octahedron

regular dodecahedron   regular icosahedron

relation symbol A symbol used to express a relationship between two quantities.

repeating decimal A decimal in which one digit or a group of digits is repeated without end. For example, 0.3333... and $23.\overline{147} = 23.147147...$ are repeating decimals. See also *terminating decimal*.

right angle A 90° angle.

rotation A movement of a figure around a fixed point, or axis; a *turn*.

rotation symmetry A figure has rotation symmetry if it can be rotated less than a full turn around a point or an axis so that the resulting figure (the *image*) exactly matches the original figure (the *preimage*).

round To adjust a number to make it easier to work with or to make it better reflect the level of precision of the data. Often numbers are rounded to the nearest multiple of 10, 100, 1,000, and so on. For example, 12,964 rounded to the nearest thousand is 13,000.

scale (1) The *ratio* of a distance on a map, globe, or drawing to an actual distance. (2) A system of ordered marks at fixed intervals used in measurement; or any instrument that has such marks. For example, a ruler with scales in inches and centimeters, and a thermometer with scales in °F and °C. See also *scale drawing*.

scale drawing A drawing of an object or a region in which all parts are drawn to the same *scale*. Architects and builders use scale drawings.

scale factor The *ratio* of the size of a drawing or model of an object to the actual size of the object. See also *scale model* and *scale drawing*.

scale model A model of an object in which all parts are in the same proportions as in the actual object. For example, many model trains and airplanes are scale models of actual vehicles.

scientific notation A system for writing numbers in which a number is written as the product of a *power of 10* and a number that is at least 1 and less than 10. Scientific notation allows you to write big and small numbers with only a few symbols. For example, $4 * 10^{12}$ is scientific notation for 4,000,000,000,000.

sector A region bounded by an *arc* and two *radii* of a circle. The arc and 2 radii are part of the sector. A sector resembles a slice of pizza. The word *wedge* is sometimes used instead of sector.

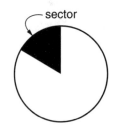
sector

side (1) One of the rays or segments that form an angle. (2) One of the line segments of a polygon. (3) One of the faces of a polyhedron.

similar Figures that have the same shape, but not necessarily the same size.

simpler form An equivalent fraction with a smaller numerator and smaller denominator. A fraction can be put in simpler form by dividing its numerator and denominator by a common factor greater than one. For example, dividing the numerator and denominator of $\frac{18}{24}$ by 2 gives the simpler form $\frac{9}{12}$.

simplest form A fraction that cannot be renamed in simpler form. Also known as *lowest terms*. A *mixed number* is in simplest form if its fractional part is in simplest form.

simplify (1) For a fraction: To express a fraction in *simpler form*. (2) For an equation or expression: To rewrite by removing parentheses and combining like terms and constants. For example, $7y + 4 + 5 + 3y$ simplifies to $10y + 9$, and $2(a + 4) = 4a + 1 + 3$ simplifies to $2a + 8 = 4a + 4$.

skew lines Lines in space that do not lie in the same plane. Skew lines *do not intersect* and are *not parallel*. For example, an east-west line on the floor and a north-south line on the ceiling are skew.

slide See *translation*.

slide rule An *Everyday Mathematics* tool used for adding and subtracting integers and fractions.

solution set The set of all solutions of an equation or inequality. For example, the solution set of $x^2 = 25$ is {5, $-$ 5} because substitution of either 5 or $-$ 5 for x makes the sentence true.

square number A number that is the product of a counting number with itself. For example, 25 is a square number because $25 = 5 * 5$. The

square numbers are 1, 4, 9, 16, 25, and so on.

square of a number The product of a number with itself. For example, 81 is the square of 9 because $81 = 9 * 9$. And 0.64 is the square of 0.8 because $0.64 = 0.8 * 0.8$.

square root of a number The square root of a number n is a number that, when multiplied by itself, gives n. For example, 4 is the square root of 16 because $4 * 4 = 16$.

square unit A unit used in measuring area, such as a square centimeter or a square foot.

standard notation The most familiar way of representing whole numbers, integers, and decimals. In standard notation, numbers are written using the *base-ten place-value* system. For example, standard notation for three hundred fifty-six is 356. See also *scientific notation* and *number-and-word notation*.

stem-and-leaf plot A display of data in which digits with larger *place values* are "stems" and digits with smaller place values are "leaves."

subtrahend In subtraction, the number being subtracted. For example, in $19 - 5 = 14$, the subtrahend is 5. See also *minuend*.

sum The result of adding two or more numbers. For example, in $5 + 3 = 8$, the sum is 8. See also *addend*.

supplementary angles Two angles whose measures total 180°.

surface area The total area of all of the surfaces that surround a 3-dimensional object.

symmetric (1) Having two parts that are mirror images of each other. (2) Looking the same when turned by some amount less than 360°. See also *point symmetry* and *rotation symmetry*.

term In an *algebraic expression*, a number or a product of a number and one or more *variables*. For example, in the expression $5y + 3k - 8$, the terms are $5y$, $3k$, and 8. The 8 is called a constant term, or simply a constant, because it has no variable part.

terminating decimal A decimal that ends. For example, 0.5 and 2.125 are terminating decimals. See also *repeating decimal*.

tessellation An arrangement of shapes that covers a surface completely without overlaps or gaps. Also called a *tiling*.

theorem A mathematical statement that can be proved to be true.

3-dimensional (3-D) Having length, width, and thickness. Solid objects take up volume and are 3-dimensional. A figure whose points are not all in a single plane is 3-dimensional.

time graph A graph that is constructed from a story that takes place over time. A time graph shows what has happened during a period of time.

trade-first subtraction method A subtraction method in which all trades are done before any subtractions are carried out.

transformation Something done to a geometric figure that produces a new figure. The most common transformations are *translations* (slides), *reflections* (flips), and *rotations* (turns).

translation A movement of a figure along a straight line; a *slide*. In a translation, each point of the figure slides the same distance in the same direction.

transversal A line that crosses two or more other lines.

tree diagram A diagram such as a *factor tree* or probability tree diagram. A tree diagram is a network of points connected by line segments. Tree diagrams can be used to factor numbers and to represent probability situations that consist of two or more choices or stages.

turn See *rotation*.

turn-around facts A pair of multiplication or addition facts in which the order of the factors (or addends) is reversed. For example, $3 * 9 = 27$ and $9 * 3 = 27$ are turn-around multiplication facts. And $4 + 5 = 9$ and $5 + 4 = 9$ are turn-around addition facts. There are no turn-around facts for division or subtraction. See also *commutative property*.

turn-around rule A rule for solving addition and multiplication problems based on the *commutative property*. For example, if you know that $6 * 8 = 48$, then, by the turn-around rule, you also know that $8 * 6 = 48$.

twin primes Two *prime numbers* that have a difference of 2. For example, 3 and 5 are twin primes, and 11 and 13 are twin primes.

2-dimensional (2-D) Having length and width but not thickness. A figure whose points are all in one plane is 2-dimensional. Circles and polygons are 2-dimensional. 2-dimensional shapes have area but not volume.

unit A label used to put a number in context. The *ONE*. In measuring length, for example, the inch and the centimeter are units. In a problem about 5 apples, *apple* is the unit. See also *whole*.

unit fraction A fraction whose numerator is 1. For example, $\frac{1}{2}, \frac{1}{3}, \frac{1}{8},$ and $\frac{1}{20}$ are unit fractions.

unit percent One percent (1%).

unlike denominators Denominators that are different, as in $\frac{1}{2}$ and $\frac{1}{3}$.

"unsquaring" a number Finding the *square root* of a number.

variable A letter or other symbol that represents a number. In the number sentence $5 + n = 9$, any number may be substituted for n, but only 4 makes the sentence true. In the inequality $x + 2 < 10$, any number may be substituted for x, but only numbers less than 8 make the sentence true. In the equation $a + 3 = 3 + a$, any number may be substituted for a, and every number makes the sentence true.

variable term A *term* that contains at least one variable.

Venn diagram A picture that uses circles or rings to show relationships between sets.

Girls on Sports Teams

track　　　basketball

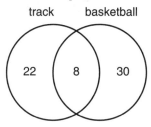

vertex (plural: **vertices**) The point where the sides of an angle, the sides of a polygon, or the edges of a polyhedron meet.

vertex point A point where corners of shapes in a *tessellation* meet.

vertical Upright; perpendicular to the horizon.

vertical (opposite) angles When two lines intersect, the angles that do not share a common side. Vertical angles have equal measures.

volume A measure of how much space a solid object takes up. Volume is measured in cubic units, such as cubic centimeters or cubic inches. The volume or capacity of a container is a measure of how much the container will hold. Capacity is measured in units such as gallons or liters.

"What's My Rule?" problem A type of problem that asks for a rule connecting two sets of numbers. Also, a type of problem that asks for one of the sets of numbers, given a rule and the other set of numbers.

whole (or ONE or unit) The entire object, collection of objects, or quantity being considered. The ONE, the *unit*, 100%.

whole numbers The *counting numbers*, together with 0. The set of whole numbers is {0, 1, 2, 3, ...}.

Administrator Ideas for Family Communication

The principal plays a key role in helping teachers, students, and parents grow together in their mathematical knowledge by making sure that each member of the school community has the right information, materials, and support. The following pages contain suggestions from experienced administrators on four key approaches to communicating with parents and promoting the benefits of *Everyday Mathematics*. The reproducible pages that follow provide materials and samples that complement these approaches.

Administrator Ideas

Sharing the Program Philosophy

As one former principal says, "If parents understand the *Everyday Mathematics* program, they will not only want their children to participate in the program, they will insist upon it!" Parents need opportunities to learn about the philosophical foundation of *Everyday Mathematics* in order to become informed supporters. Because parents learn in as many different ways as their children do, the ideas that follow use a variety of formats.

▷ Letter of Introduction

In the spring before the first year of implementation, introduce *Everyday Mathematics* in a letter to parents. You may want to describe key features of the program, reasons for its adoption, and ways to find out more about *Everyday Mathematics* (sample letter on p. 97). You may also attach a copy of A Curriculum for the 21st Century (pp. 98 and 99) to give parents a background for understanding the philosophy of the program. Include similar information in a "welcome back" letter as well.

▷ Newsletter Notes

Throughout the school year, it's helpful to include short, informative notes about *Everyday Mathematics* in your school newsletters. You may want to write about the role of games, the interwoven design of the curriculum, assessment, or ways to help students at home. Many principals like to share anecdotes about impressive things they've overheard or seen in their visits to classrooms—they say actual "kid stories" have a much greater impact on parents' feelings about the program than their own words do.

▷ PTA Meetings or Parent Coffees

Informative presentations (from 15–60 minutes) at evening PTA meetings, daytime coffees, or teas are good ways to connect with busy parents. Make a point of scheduling several of these throughout the school year, especially if *Everyday Mathematics* is new to your school. (See Sample Parent Orientation Schedule, page 101.) You can share the program philosophy through overhead transparencies of materials in this handbook, such as Developing Mathematical Literacy on page 100. It's even better to invite several students to share an activity, game, or

> "**To show** parents the scope of the curriculum, we display a series of strand traces in the front foyer. For Open House we presented, "Tracing Geometry through the Grades with Everyday Mathematics." *This is a great introductory strand trace because it breaks down geometry into concepts, and the 3-dimensional objects attached make for a lively display. We put up an Algebra strand trace for fall parent conferences, and a Statistics and Probability display for spring conferences.*"
>
> **Penny Williams**
> **Math Support Teacher**
> **Anchorage School District**
> **Anchorage, Alaska**

project they've done in the classroom. One principal likes to have students explain their unique solutions to a common problem to demonstrate the benefits of problem solving and alternative algorithms. (See Problems that Invite Multiple Solutions, pages 103 and 104.)

▷ Parent Handbook

Familiarize parents with the program and empower them to help their children by creating an *Everyday Mathematics* Parent Handbook. Consider whether you want to have an all-school handbook or whether you'd like teachers to create grade-specific handbooks. Use the materials in this book for the contents and include an introduction explaining some of the ways interested parents can learn more—the UCSMP Web site, everydaymath.uchicago.edu, is a great reference.

> *"We know that parents want to be involved in their children's education, so our district created an* Everyday Mathematics *K–6 Parent Handbook. This handbook includes our district and state math goals, a program overview, explanations of program routines and concepts, a glossary of the mathematical terms, a list of literature that supports the* Everyday Mathematics *content strands, and directions for many of the games."*
>
> **Sandy Schoff**
> **Pre K–12 Mathematics**
>   **Coordinator**
> **Anchorage School**
>   **District**
> **Anchorage, Alaska**

▷ Displays

Bulletin boards and walls of your school and main office can serve as "information centers". Show parents how concepts or skills are developed across the grades by using a bulletin board to display a visual strand trace created by teachers (p. 106). Ask teachers at each grade level to save products from activities related to that strand during a certain time period, for example, the first month of school. Create a title, such as "Developing Measurement Skills, Pre-K–6" and display students' work in grade-level order. Add a brief caption to remind parents of the philosophy behind the products, such as "In *Everyday Mathematics*, students learn to use measurement tools and different units of measure to solve meaningful problems." You can also create displays that feature projects or answer questions, such as "What Is Problem Solving?"

▷ Report Cards

If your school has revised its report cards as a result of adopting *Everyday Mathematics*, you will want to explain the reasons for any change in advance. Ideally, changes in assessment or year-end goals can be brought up early by teachers during parent-teacher conferences, but report cards are also a good topic for a Parent Coffee or a PTA presentation. Since it never hurts to repeat information several times, you could address such changes in your school newsletter. It is important to note that most principals do not recommend changing the report card until your school has been implementing the program for more than one year.

Providing Program Experiences

Give parents an opportunity to learn by doing. This will not only deepen their understanding and appreciation of the program, it will make them advocates and possibly eager volunteers.

▷ Games at Home

It is important for parents to understand the purpose of the *Everyday Mathematics* games. One of the best ways to develop parents' appreciation of the games is to have them play several with their children at home. If your district adopts the program in the spring for next fall, have teachers introduce a few *Everyday Mathematics* games to students during the end of the school year prior to implementation. These games can be sent home in the form of "summer fun" kits for families to enjoy together. Have teams of parent volunteers put the kits together, being sure to include the game's target objectives and concepts along with the directions. If you are short on time, consider buying Family Games Kits which contain games already ready to send home.

During the school year, encourage teachers to assign games to be played at home for independent practice. You might even have an all-school "*Top-It* Week*" (perfect for National TV-Turnoff Week) where all students play a grade-appropriate version of this game with their parents and report the results! Be sure to quote students or include their own written stories in your newsletter.

▷ Family Math Nights

Bringing families and students together for a special *Everyday Mathematics* event requires extra planning and organization, but the positive impact on parents' understanding and support of the program make the effort worthwhile. At a Family Math Night, parents can rotate through various instructional stations (often led by students), view displays, try out the *Everyday Mathematics* technology, participate in question-and-answer sessions, or make a tool or game to use at home. (See pages 59–65 for planning support.) Think about focusing the event on a single strand to show how concepts develop across the grades; this is especially appropriate if your staff has completed a strand trace. (See page 106.)

> *"Parent support is essential to systemic change in mathematics. To help parents provide this much-needed support, the Office of Mathematics uses a parent curriculum designed by the Mathematics Education Collaborative to provide workshops for parents and parent liaisons so that they better understand mathematics content and the standards-based pedagogy of Everyday Mathematics."*
>
> **May L. Samuels**
> **Director of**
>   **Mathematics**
> **Newark Public Schools**
> **Newark, New Jersey**

Administrator Ideas

▷ Observers or Volunteers

Get parents into classrooms to see *Everyday Mathematics* in action and, better yet, turn them into helpers! Some of your best advocates will be parents who see engaged students, relevant lessons, and rigorous mathematical content firsthand. Your teachers will appreciate any boost you can give to rounding up a few volunteers—you might consider passing out the volunteer form (p. 68) when you greet parents in the morning or meet with them to answer questions. In first through third grades, parent help with Explorations can be a huge asset, especially to teachers in the first year of implementation. In order to head-off the parents' concern that "I don't know anything about this kind of math," hold confidence-building workshops.

▷ Workshops for Parents

Schools with supportive families often offer opportunities for parents to learn aspects of *Everyday Mathematics* themselves, such as routines, games, and alternative algorithms. (See Sample Algorithm Workshop Schedule, page 102.) "Lunch-and-Learn" and conference day workshops are often convenient for working parents. The leader of the workshop—you, a math coordinator, or a teacher—should use a friendly "this-was-new-to-me-too" tone, and encourage parents to help each other and share questions and insights. Materials in this handbook can serve as handouts or teach lessons directly from the *Teacher's Lesson Guide*. After the first year of implementation, consider having a core group of dedicated and reliable parent volunteers help run the workshops.

> *"At our Family Math Night, we gave each family member a passport. After they played a game, they received a stamp on their passport. After receiving four stamps and completing a simple evaluation form, parents turned in their passports for a free dinner at the Family Math Night and were eligible for prize drawings. Each winner selected a copy of one of the games that were played during the evening. We had a representative available to address any concerns regarding the* Everyday Mathematics *program. Very few parents had questions and we took that as a good sign that they are pleased with the program."*

Francesca Blueher
Elementary School
   Teacher/Math Leader
Albuquerque Public Schools
Albuquerque, NM

Using Resources and Research

For most parents, *Everyday Mathematics* is quite different from the math program they grew up with. As a principal, you will want to reassure parents that *Everyday Mathematics* is an educationally-sound program that will enable their children to succeed in mathematics. You will also want to track your students' performance so that you can, indeed, verify their achievements. Here are some ways to use resources and research in communicating about *Everyday Mathematics* with your school's parent community.

▷ UCSMP Online Resources

The University of Chicago School Mathematics Project has a Web site for educators, parents, and students. At everydaymath.uchicago.edu, go to the Educator's Homeroom to find program development information, research papers, implementation stories, and even a museum of student products.

▷ Published Research

As you and your staff read professional journals, look for articles and papers that review research on how students learn mathematics, effective instructional practices, problem solving, and skills development. Copy articles that support the philosophy and practices of *Everyday Mathematics*, and collect them in a binder. You can pull material from this binder for newsletters, presentations, or parent inquiries, or keep the binder in a prominent place in the office for parents to view.

▷ *Success Stories*

Invite other schools or districts to share their *Everyday Mathematics* success stories with your parent community. There are many schools and districts who are long-term, enthusiastic users and supporters of *Everyday Mathematics* who would be happy to discuss their program experiences. In addition, the publisher of *Everyday Mathematics* has available a number of informative papers that may help you promote the curriculum. Ask your area *Everyday Mathematics* representative for *Student Achievement Studies I–V*. You may also want to request several *Success Stories*— written "snapshots" of schools and districts around the country that have had positive results using the program. In these *Success Stories*, the school or district's process of selecting and implementing *Everyday Mathematics* is described and long-term student achievement data indicating positive results on various state tests is presented. You can find these stories at www.wrightgroup.com.

> *"The best research to use to promote* Everyday Mathematics *is your own. As soon as you receive your first test results, get the data out to parents."*
>
> **Janice L. Haake**
> **Director of Curriculum**
> **and Instruction PreK–5**
> **Plainfield CCSD #202**
> **Plainfield, IL**

▷ State Standards

Use your state learning standards to highlight the strengths of *Everyday Mathematics*. In your newsletter or in a short presentation, identify one of the state goals or standards for mathematics, and describe how it is addressed in *Everyday Mathematics*. For example, if the goal is for students to "reason mathematically by gathering data, analyzing evidence, and building arguments to support or refute hypotheses," you might describe the Daily Routines, begun as early as Kindergarten, that involve data collection and display— the Survey Routine, Weather and Temperature Routines, Attendance, and so on. Describe a few key data-related activities that appear in subsequent grades. You can also show this alignment visually using any *Content by Strand* Poster. Print the goal or standard on brightly-colored paper and hang it above the poster. Use colored stick-on "flags" to mark all the places along the strand where this goal is addressed.

> "*At the* entrance to our school, we have a Data and Curriculum Board to keep parents informed of current data—both summative and formative data concerning the achievement and growth of students. I made a graph in Excel that contains test scores from the past two years to show our growth. Teachers also submit various data and graphs to show how their classes have been improving in literacy as well as mathematics. Some of the graphs displayed on the board are generated by students!"
>
> **Dr. Dwain Arnold**
> **Principal**
> **Kingsport City Schools**
> **Kingsport, TN**

▷ Your School Data

Display your school's student achievement data in charts or graphs for your staff and parent community to see how students are performing. Graphs can be made easily from data entered into a spreadsheet program—experiment with different types of graphs to see which best conveys the information of interest. The examples in Displaying School Data (p. 110) will give you some ideas.

Administrator Ideas

Supporting Staff

Because classroom teachers are "on the front line" of parent communication, they must be positive and knowledgeable about *Everyday Mathematics*. One of the best ways to assure that your parent community responds positively to the program is to provide ongoing support for teachers.

▷ Proactive Communication

When *Everyday Mathematics* is new to your school, teachers may not be sure how to respond to parents' questions or concerns until they have had some experience with the program. Meet with teachers to brainstorm questions that might be raised, and discuss how to best answer them. After your first year of implementation, continue to make parent communication a regular topic at staff meetings, as subsequent years may bring new questions and concerns.

▷ Staff Meetings that Count

Establish a plan for ongoing staff development that includes regular use of staff meetings for *Everyday Mathematics*-related discussions and activities. (See Staff Meeting Topics and Activities, page 105, for ideas.) If your teachers do not have grade-level planning time, try to give them time to plan and share successes and challenges throughout the year. Many principals feel that using staff meeting time to complete a "strand trace" is valuable. They have teachers work together, first in grade-level groups and then across the grades, to see how a certain concept or skill in one strand is developed in each grade.

▷ Classroom Observations

Create a learning community of teachers by helping teachers observe each other's classes during mathematics. Some principals make this happen by teaching math in one class while the teacher observes in another class. Others hire a "floating" substitute to relieve one teacher every hour for observation. (In this case, teachers must stagger their math times.) Commit to giving observations high priority by planning and scheduling them several times throughout the year.

▷ Classroom Set-up

Setting up a classroom can be daunting to new teachers or teachers new to *Everyday Mathematics*. Provide teachers with the

> *"For new teachers or teachers new to a grade level, we provide unit-by-unit professional development throughout the year. These professional development days focus on the content of the units and the* Everyday Mathematics *lesson design, so that teachers understand the importance of each lesson and the sequence of lessons and units."*
>
> **Yvonne Comer-Holbrook**
> **Mathematics Resource**
> **Teacher**
> **Pittsburgh Public Schools**
> **Pittsburgh, PA**

Classroom Set-up Guide, pages 107–109, before school begins so they know what to display and prepare. Some principals even post a guide like this on their teachers' doors. If teachers follow this guide, they will complete most of their *Everyday Mathematics* preparation for Back-to-School Night.

▷ Teacherlink and the UCSMP Listserve

Users of *Everyday Mathematics* can receive the network newsletter, Teacherlink®, which includes articles written by teachers, administrators, and the UCSMP authors. Subscribe by writing to Teacherlink, P.O. Box 812960, Chicago, IL 60601. The UCSMP Web site also sponsors an e-mail discussion group. To join the group, follow the directions in the Educator's Homeroom under Forums at everydaymath.uchicago.edu.

▷ *Everyday Mathematics*-related Professional Development

Professional development raises teachers' excitement and enthusiasm about the program. The www.teacherhelp.com Web site lists many professional development opportunities available for *Everyday Mathematics* users. Consider sending teachers to *Everyday Mathematics* summer conference or schedule onsite professional development in your school.

Once your teachers have been with *Everyday Mathematics* for a couple of years and have a firm grasp of the management, providing workshops that deepen their content knowledge is quite beneficial.

> *"Our quarterly staff e-newsletter helps keep faculty informed of what should be occurring in the* Everyday Mathematics *classrooms. In it, they can find reminders, suggestions, helpful Web sites, workshop offerings, parent advice, organizational tips, pacing, and FCAT information, as well as highlights from our Math Specialist Trainings."*

Kerry Tastinger
Math Lab Instructor/
Math Specialist
Orange County
Public Schools
Orlando, FL

Curtis Yarbrough
Math Lab Instructor/
Math Specialist
Orange County
Public Schools
Orlando, FL

▷ Teacher Knowledge

Teachers are able to use *Everyday Mathematics* more confidently and effectively when they understand the research upon which the program philosophy is based. This research is explained in an engaging, easy-to-read interview with the developer of *Everyday Mathematics*, Max Bell, which can be found at www2.edc.org/mcc/images/perspeverydaymath.pdf. You might have teachers read this article, then discuss informally. In addition, help teachers stay up-to-date on instructional practices and research in the field by subscribing to and circulating one or more of the educational journals. There is a list of such resources at everydaymath.uchicago.edu in the section for educators.

Administrator Masters for Family Communication

In addition to material included in the teacher section of this handbook, the following pages can be used to carry out many of the ideas presented earlier. Notice that the sample introductory letter is meant to serve as a model for your own letter and is not intended to be reproduced.

Administrator Masters

To assist you with distributing these reproducible forms, please look for one of the following icons at the top of each page.

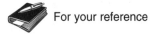 For your reference

 Materials to send home

Sample Letter of Introduction

Dear Parents:

I am pleased to announce the district's recent adoption of *Everyday Mathematics* for Grades Pre-K through 6. In the fall of 2007, teachers and students will begin using this research-based curriculum, developed as part of the University of Chicago School Mathematics Project (UCSMP). *Everyday Mathematics* reflects the state and national goals for mathematics and includes these features:

- ◆ A curriculum that explores mathematical content beyond basic arithmetic
- ◆ A problem-solving approach based on everyday situations
- ◆ Frequent, varied practice of basic skills
- ◆ An instructional approach that revisits concepts regularly
- ◆ An emphasis on communication and teamwork
- ◆ A commitment to home/school partnerships

In the past few decades, there has been a tremendous increase in the importance of mathematics in the workplace and daily life. In order to succeed in this information- and technology-oriented environment, our students need to learn a range of sophisticated mathematical knowledge that extends far beyond basic calculation skills. *Everyday Mathematics* is a program that will prepare students for the future and enable them to achieve at high levels.

If you would like to learn more about *Everyday Mathematics*, please attend a **Parent Orientation on June 5, 7:00 P.M.–8:00 P.M.**, or browse the Parent's Homeroom on the UCSMP Web site at everydaymath.uchicago.edu. You will also be able to become acquainted with the math games that are a key component of basic skills practice in *Everyday Mathematics*, as all students will bring home a Family Games Kit for the summer.

We are excited about the adoption of *Everyday Mathematics* and feel confident that this program will make the study of mathematics an engaging, enriching, and successful experience for all students.

Principal

School Name

A Curriculum for the 21st Century

The goal of the University of Chicago Mathematics Project is to significantly improve the mathematics curriculum and instruction being offered to school students in the U.S. The *Everyday Mathematics* curriculum was developed as part of this mission.

▷ Philosophy of *Everyday Mathematics*

The philosophy of the program is based on extensive research about how students learn mathematics and how mathematics is taught. Students need a rigorous and balanced mathematics curriculum. Such a curriculum:

- **emphasizes conceptual understanding while building a mastery of basic skills.** When students understand mathematics, rather than simply memorize facts or procedures, they are able to use their knowledge flexibly and solve new and unfamiliar problems.

- **explores the full mathematics spectrum, not just basic arithmetic.** Students are introduced to all major mathematical content areas—number sense, algebra, measurement, geometry, data analysis, and probability—beginning in Kindergarten.

- **considers how students learn, what they're interested in, and the future for which they must be prepared.** Consistent with the ways students actually learn mathematics, the program allows for understanding to be built over time. Students acquire knowledge and skills through active involvement in meaningful, real world experiences.

Everyday Mathematics was developed through a process of writing, field testing, and revising one grade level at a time. The result is a comprehensive Pre-K through Grade 6 curriculum that carefully builds upon and extends knowledge and skills from one year to the next.

▷ Outstanding Features of the *Everyday Mathematics* Curriculum

- **Real-life Problem Solving**
  Students learn and use mathematics in real-world situations. Activities and lessons explore a wide variety of mathematical content, such as geometry, probability, and algebra, in contexts that are interesting to students and worthy of their time and attention.

- **Balanced Instruction**
  Lessons include whole-group instruction, as well as small group, partner, or individual activities. There is a balance of teacher-directed instruction and open-ended, hands-on exploration, projects, and on-going practice.

- ◆ **Carefully Planned, Sequenced Instruction**

  Instruction builds on the intuitive, concrete knowledge and abilities of young students and gradually helps them develop an understanding of the abstract and symbolic. There is repeated exposure to concepts and skills, which build on each other and are highly interconnected.

- ◆ **Ongoing, Continuous Basic Skills Practice**

  Certain skills must be mastered in order to be a flexible problem solver. The program provides multiple methods for helping students practice basic skills and math facts, including games designed specifically for this purpose.

- ◆ **Emphasis on Communication**

  Students are encouraged to discuss their mathematical thinking and actively listen to each other. Teachers guide student understanding through questions and clarifications and help students learn to make logical mathematical arguments.

- ◆ **Appropriate Use of Technology**

  Students learn when and how to use technology responsibly. Technology can enable students to work at higher levels, it can help them test ideas, and it can benefit those students with special needs.

- ◆ **Home and School Partnership**

  Optimal learning involves the student, the teacher, and the home. Frequent letters keep parents informed about topics and terms being learned, and Home Links/Study Links offer opportunities to help students with review and practice.

> **Everyday Mathematics** *is committed to helping students become capable and flexible mathematical thinkers and problem solvers, which will prepare them for success in our ever-changing world.*

Developing Mathematical Literacy

In the information- and technology-based environment in which we now live, it is important for students to achieve mathematical literacy. People who are "mathematically literate" have a range of sophisticated mathematical knowledge and skills that extends far beyond basic calculation skills.

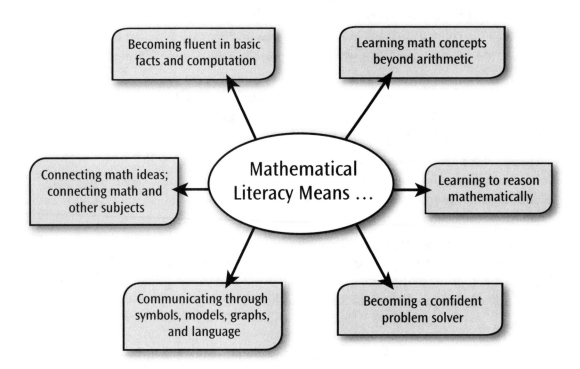

Everyday Mathematics lays the groundwork for mathematical literacy at an early age. Concepts and skills are informally introduced in the early childhood program, then revisited, developed, and extended as students progress through the grades. Increasingly-sophisticated content can be introduced at each grade level because of the carefully-planned sequence of instruction.

Sample Parent Orientation Schedule

Beginning of the Year (60 minutes total)

Time	Activity	Materials
5 minutes	Welcome, introductions, and agenda	Name tags Refreshments
15 minutes	Have participants complete an *Everyday Mathematics* lesson routine: • Name-collection boxes • Frames and Arrows • "What's My Rule?" • Math Message • Other Invite participants to share solutions. Briefly explain how this routine fits into the program.	Overhead transparency or chart paper to record solutions
15 minutes	Explain district adoption process and three reasons for selecting *Everyday Mathematics*. Share program philosophy and features.	A Curriculum for the 21st Century (pp. 98 and 99)
15 minutes	Show student materials. Explain that the *Student Math Journal* is used in class. Discuss program components as needed, such as: • Routines • Skills practice (Mental Math and Reflexes, Math Boxes, games, and Fact Triangles) • Home Links/Study Links • Family Letters • Explorations/Projects • Algorithms • *Student Reference Book/ My Reference Book*	An *Everyday Mathematics* Lesson (p. 22) Examples of these components
5 minutes	Suggest ways parents can help their children. Distribute your school's Parent Handbook.	How to Help Your Child with Mathematics (pp. 46 and 47) Handbook (optional)
5 minutes	Questions and answers Evaluation/questionnaire and/or volunteer form Thank participants for attending.	Copies of an evaluation form (p. 65) and/or volunteer form (p. 68)

Sample Algorithm Workshop Schedule

Middle of the Year (60 minutes total)

Plan to teach algorithms for no more than two operations in each workshop. Photocopies of pages 28–37 in this handbook can help explain and provide examples of algorithms.

Time	Activity	Materials
5 minutes	Welcome, introductions, and agenda	Name tags Refreshments
15 minutes	Discuss the use of algorithms in everyday situations and define *algorithm*. Share authors' philosophy of learning and using algorithms. Explain the reason for focus algorithms. Have participants calculate a 15% tip on a $75.00 bill and share their different solution strategies. Discuss how showing solutions benefits students.	Algorithms in *Everyday Mathematics*, pp. 28–37 Overhead transparency or chart paper
20 minutes	Model using the focus algorithm with a sample problem. Have participants try using the focus algorithm with another problem. Have participants explain to a partner why the algorithm works. Repeat the same method above for another operation's algorithm. (optional) Discuss the importance of Mental Math and Reflexes and automaticity with basic facts. Share ways the program encourages fact practice. Briefly show Fact Triangles or an appropriate game.	Select a problem from pp. 30–37 or use the *Teacher's Lesson Guide*. Show some examples of Mental Math and Reflexes and Fact Triangles on the overhead.
10 minutes	Have participants share advantages they see to students being exposed to different algorithms or inventing their own. Ask participants to use their new expertise as classroom volunteers!	Overhead or chart paper to record responses Volunteer form at back of room (p. 68)
10 minutes	Questions and answers Thank participants for attending.	

Problems that Invite Multiple Solutions

When parents see several students correctly solving the same problem in different ways, they begin to appreciate the reasons for developing students' conceptual understanding, their ability to think flexibly, and their enthusiasm for sharing strategies with each other. As part of an informational meeting or Family Math Night, invite a small group of students to show and explain their solutions to one or two of these problems.

Ask students to complete their problems in advance, and make an overhead transparency of their solutions. Have a collection of math tools available to help students explain their strategies—a number grid, number line, base-10 blocks, pennies, paper for drawing, and so on.

The grade level in which each problem appears is shown.

G1	G1	G1	G1
Carly has 12 pennies. Maria has 20 pennies. Who has more? How much more?	At the museum store, I bought a ball for 35¢ and an eraser for 17¢. How much did I spend?	⬜ 25 ▢	▢ ▢ 64 ▢ ▢
G2	**G2**	**G2**	**G2**
There are 10 children: $\frac{1}{2}$ play baseball, $\frac{3}{10}$ jump rope, and $\frac{1}{5}$ skate. How many children play each game?	If 10¢ is ONE, what is 5¢? What is 20¢?	$3.74 + $0.27	87 − 39
G3	**G3**	**G3**	**G3**
Share $15 among 4 people.	26 × 34	Jack earned $12. He bought a can of tennis balls that cost $\frac{1}{3}$ of his earnings. How much does he have left?	Laurel had 30 pennies. She put 12 pennies in her bank and gave the other pennies to three friends. How many pennies did each friend get?

G4 The senior class at Rees High School raised $1,895 to share equally among 5 local charities. How much money will each charity receive?	**G4** Martin brought 18 quarters to the arcade. He spent $\frac{1}{2}$ of the quarters on video games and $\frac{1}{3}$ of them on Skeet-ball. How much money did he spend on video games? On Skeet-ball? How much money did he have left?	**G4** $\quad\quad 18$ $\quad\quad 420$ $\quad\quad 120$ $+\ 2,800$	**G4** ___ = 3 * 470
G5 Here is an up-and-down staircase that is 5 steps tall. How many squares are needed for an up-and-down staircase that is 10 steps tall? 50 steps tall? 	**G5** What is the area of triangle *ABC*? 	**G5** Divide 600 by 22.	**G5** 15.2 * 3.6 =
G6 On average, a person needs to consume $2\frac{1}{2}$ quarts of water a day. At this rate, about how many quarts of water would a person consume in 1 year?	**G6** Marta's mother is 5 times as old as Marta. Marta's mother is 25. How old is Marta? In a few years, Marta's mother will be 3 times as old as Marta. What will their ages be then?	**G6** Solve mentally. 60% of 45. Explain the strategy you used.	**G6** 36)4,537

Staff Meeting Topics and Activities

This wide range of topics and activities will help you make *Everyday Mathematics* a regular part of staff meetings. Even after your first year of implementation, teachers benefit from having meaningful discussions and doing informative activities with their colleagues.

Discussion Topics	Activities
☐ Classroom set-up	☐ Visit classrooms of experienced *Everyday Mathematics* teachers.
☐ Management tips	
☐ Manipulatives	☐ Work in groups or grade level meetings to plan pacing of lessons; mark the *Teacher's Lesson Guide* by quarters.
☐ How's it going? (Q & A)	
☐ Parent concerns	
☐ Parent education	
☐ Routines: why and how	☐ Have grade level teachers meet with the grades above and below them to learn what the curriculum is covering before and after their grade levels.
☐ Pacing of lessons	
☐ Content by strands	
☐ Differentiating instruction	
☐ Family Letters and Home/ Study Links	☐ Compile material for a Parent Handbook.
☐ Parent handbook	☐ Share ways to keep observational records, assessment notes, and checklists.
☐ *Minute Math®+/ 5-Minute Math*	
☐ Games in the classroom	☐ Share student work on Open Response problems and practice scoring with a rubric.
☐ Games at home	
☐ Ongoing assessment	☐ Review current report card and problem solve if modifications are required.
☐ Periodic assessment	
☐ Open Response questions and rubrics	☐ Have grade levels teach each other games.
☐ Portfolios	☐ Share portfolios from several classrooms; discuss how they're used with students and families.
☐ Back-to-School Night	
☐ Conferences	
☐ Report cards	☐ Strand Trace: Grade-level (p. 106)
☐ Family Math Night	☐ Strand Trace: Games (p. 106)
☐ Parent volunteers	☐ Strand Trace: Cross-grade (p. 106)
☐ Summer plans	
☐ Projects/Explorations	
☐ Mathematical content	

Strand Trace Activities for Staff Development

Strand Trace Activities familiarize teachers with the curriculum and reassure them that the sequence of instruction is sound. Teachers come to see how concepts are revisited, how practice is distributed, and how mastery is achieved over time. Several strand trace plans are described below, and many principals use all three over the course of several years.

Particularly good strands and concepts to trace:

Number and Numeration: Place Value

Operations and Computation: Algorithms and Computation

Data and Chance: Charts and Graphs

Measurement and Reference Frames: Volume/Capacity/Weight

Geometry: Angles and Rotations

Patterns, Functions, and Algebra: Sequences

Plan 1: Grade-Level Groups—*especially good for new users*

- Teachers gather with grade-level colleagues.
- Teachers identify lessons/activities where concept is introduced, revisited, or practiced (including games).
- Teachers draw pictures to represent activities, arranging them sequentially (taped to wall, glued on chart paper).
- Concluding discussion: In what different contexts do students experience this concept? How is mastery developed?

Plan 2: Cross-Grade Game Share—*good for all*

- Prior to meeting: One concept/skill is selected for the Game Share.
- Each grade identifies a game that develops the selected concept.
- At the meeting: Teachers sit in cross-grade groupings and teach each other their games.
- If not all grade levels have time to share, distribute this activity throughout several meetings, with two grades sharing per meeting.
- Concluding discussion: How does the conceptual understanding or skill involved in playing each game change from grade to grade?

Plan 3: Cross-Grade Strand Trace—*good for experienced users*

- Teachers complete Plan 1 for a grade other than their own or try a strand trace for all the grades.
- Concluding discussion: How do the activities in this grade level build on (or build a foundation for) the concepts or skills learned by students at your own grade level? If the staff chooses to trace a strand Pre-K–6, discuss how the concepts build from each grade level and how seeing this development should help teachers with pacing.

Classroom Set-up Guide: Kindergarten

Welcome back! Before you plan your first week and set up your classroom, read over the initial sections of your *Teacher's Guide to Activities* (*TGA*) and *Teacher's Reference Manual* (*TRM*). There are many items that you'll need to display on your classroom walls and some materials you'll need to make or gather. Take time to prepare the items on this list that you find helpful. If you laminate the items, you'll be able to re-use them year after year.

☐ Read through the initial sections of the *TRM* for a description of the classroom mathematical environment you'll want to create. Start planning a general schedule that will incorporate the Ongoing Daily Routines.

☐ Arrange your classroom: consider space for whole-group activities, small-group activities (centers), partner work, and individual explorations.

☐ Prepare for the Ongoing Daily Routines as described in the *TGA*:

- Job Chart
- Growing Number Line (at child height)
- Calendar
- Temperature
- Attendance
- Weather
- Daily Schedule

☐ Consult the list of materials and supplies in the *TGA* and begin gathering materials.

☐ Start a list of supplies for children to bring from home—coins, containers, magazines, bottle caps, and so on.

☐ Read and prepare any materials needed for the first week of Section 1 in the *TGA*.

☐ Review the different theme ideas in *Resources for the Kindergarten Classroom* to see if there are any activities you might like to use at the beginning of the year.

☐ Prepare a flip-card clipboard or other system for recording observations as described in your *Assessment Handbook*. Read about Ongoing Assessment.

☐ Prepare a letter for home—explain that children will learn math by doing math, describe some of the daily routines, encourage parent involvement.

☐ Consider photocopying all Activity Masters and Home Links and storing in files.

Classroom Set-up Guide: Grades 1 through 3

Welcome back! Before you plan your first week and set up your classroom, read over the initial sections of your *Everyday Mathematics Teacher's Lesson Guide* (*TLG*) and *Teacher's Reference Manual* (*TRM*). There are many items that you'll need to display on your classroom walls and some materials you'll need to make or gather. Take time to prepare the items on this list that you find helpful. If you laminate the items, you'll be able to re-use them year after year.

☐ Read the Management Guide in your *TRM* for a description of the routines and classroom set up. Start planning a daily math schedule that includes morning routines, lessons, and games.

☐ Arrange classroom desks/tables for flexible groupings, efficient transitions, easy access to manipulatives, space for math center(s), and so on.

☐ Read over the first unit, including the Unit Organizer. If children create a "Museum" in this unit, reserve a bulletin board or wall space.

☐ Obtain a starting supply of paper (6–7 sheets of each kind per child): plain paper or newsprint ($8\frac{1}{2}" \times 1"$), primary-grade handwriting paper, construction paper, graph paper (1-inch grid, plus $\frac{1}{2}$-inch grid for third grade).

☐ Obtain a large pad of newsprint for a Class Data Pad.

☐ Make number cards with number words. (Use index cards, laminate.)

☐ Mark the directions N, S, E, W in the classroom.

☐ Display a number line (–35 to 180) and the Number Grid poster.

☐ Decide on a calendar format. (See the *TRM*.)

☐ Prepare weather/temperature recording charts and class thermometer. (See the *TRM*.)

☐ Choose a Tool Kit storage device such as zippered bags or plastic envelopes, and number each kit. Create a lost-and-found box for Tool Kit manipulatives.

☐ Put together a collection of pennies (10 per student).

☐ Decide how and where slates, chalk, and so on, will be stored.

☐ Make a "Working with a Partner" or "Partnership Principles" poster. (See the *TRM*.)

☐ Start a supplies list for children to bring from home—socks, coins, and so on.

☐ Prepare an in-box (or other place) where children can deposit written work, such as Math Messages and Home Links.

☐ Consider photocopying all Math Masters (especially Home Links) and storing them in files.

Classroom Set-up Guide: Grades 4 through 6

Welcome back! Before you plan your first week and set up your classroom, read over the initial sections of your *Everyday Mathematics Teacher's Lesson Guide (TLG)* and *Teacher's Reference Manual (TRM)*. There are many items that you'll need to display on your classroom walls and some materials you'll need to make or gather. Take time to prepare the items on this list that you find helpful. If you laminate the items, you'll be able to re-use them year after year.

☐ Read the Management Guide in your *TRM* for a description of the routines and classroom set up. Start planning a daily math schedule that includes routines, lessons, ongoing practice, and games.

☐ Arrange classroom desks/tables for flexible groupings, efficient transitions, easy access to manipulatives, space for math center(s), and so on.

☐ Read over the first unit, including the Unit Organizer. If students create a "Museum" in this unit, reserve a bulletin board or wall space.

☐ Obtain a starting supply of paper for the year (6–7 sheets of each kind per student): plain paper or newsprint ($8\frac{1}{2}$" × 1"), construction paper, centimeter graph paper.

☐ Obtain a large pad of newsprint for a Class Data Pad.

☐ Mark the directions N, S, E, W in the classroom.

☐ Display a number line (−35 to 180).

☐ Display grade-specific posters, such as Probability Meter or Real Number Line.

☐ Choose a Tool Kit storage device such as zippered bags, plastic envelopes, and so forth. Write identification numbers on kits and certain tools (calculators, templates, and so on).

☐ Create a lost-and-found box for Tool Kit manipulatives.

☐ Decide how and where slates, chalk, and so on will be stored.

☐ Make a "Partnership Principles" poster. (See the *TRM*.)

☐ Prepare an in-box (or other place) where students can deposit written work, such as Math Messages and Study Links.

☐ Consider photocopying all Math Masters (especially Study Links) and storing them in files.

Displaying School Data

A graph comparing your students' achievement to state-wide achievement is one of the most effective ways to share data with parents. Follow these steps to create a graph using popular database/spreadsheet software in under 30 minutes.

1) Decide What to Communicate

Look over your school and state data, and think through these questions:

◆ What strikes you most about this data? What should parents notice?

◆ Do you want to communicate information about *all* students or only those students meeting or exceeding a certain level of proficiency?

2) Organize the Data

Use your spreadsheet program to do the following:

◆ Create a new worksheet. Use years (2007, 2008, and so on) as column labels. Use your school name and "State Total" as row labels.

◆ Enter the data from your school and the state. Add a title. (See examples below.)

3) Select Chart Type

Click on the type of graph that will display your data most effectively. The type of graph you choose depends on what you want to communicate.

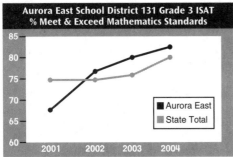

Use this type of graph to show dramatic increases, where your students' scores have improved year to year and surpassed the state scores.

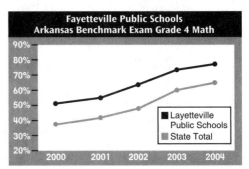

Line graphs can also be used to show a consistent higher-than-average student performance that has steadily risen.

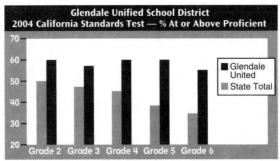

Use this type of graph when your students consistently rank above the state average. This type of graph is best for highlighting great differences rather than dramatic change over time.